Studies in Lucian

Studies in Lucian

Barry Baldwin

Hakkert
Toronto
1973

Cover design by R. Mitchell Design
Book design by Anya Humphrey

This book has been published with the help of a grant from the Humanities
Research Council of Canada, using funds provided by the Canada Council.

International Standard Book Number 0-88866-524-5
Library of Congress Catalogue Card Number 73-83516

A. M. Hakkert Ltd.
554 Spadina Crescent,
Toronto, Canada M5S 2J9

Printed and bound in Canada by the Hunter Rose Company

Contents

Acknowledgements

The paramount needs of a scholar are money and a good typist: I have been doubly fortunate.

My thanks are due to the Canada Council for a grant which enabled me to spend the summer of 1969 in London at the British Museum and Institute for Classical Studies.

Miss Jean Blodgett, Secretary to the Department of Classics at this University, has typed my manuscript with efficiency and humour. Faced with my execrable English and Greek scripts, it is hard to say which is the more astonishing of these attributes.

Barry Baldwin
University of Calgary,
Calgary, Alberta, Canada

Abbreviations and Bibliography

The following list contains the references cited and abbreviated in the foregoing pages. (*RE* articles and reviews are omitted.)

Africa, T. W., "The Opium Addiction of Marcus Aurelius," *Journal of the History of Ideas* 22, 1961, pp. 97-102.

Allegro, J. M., *The Sacred Mushroom and the Cross*, London, 1970.

Allinson, *Lucian* = Allinson, F. G., *Lucian: Satirist and Artist*, New York, 1927.

Allinson, F. G., "Pseudo-Ionicism in the Second Century A.D.," *American Journal of Philology* 7, 1886, pp. 203-17.

Arnott, P. D., "The Alphabetic Tragedy of Callias," *Classical Philology* 55, 1960, pp. 178-80.

Avenarius = Avenarius, G., *Lukians Schrift Zur Geschichtesschreibung*, Meisenheim, 1956.

Bagnani, G., "Peregrinus Proteus and the Christians," *Historia* 4, 1955, pp. 107-12.

Baldwin 1961 = Baldwin, B., "Lucian as Social Satirist," *Classical Quarterly* 11, 1961, pp. 199-208.

Baldwin 1962 = Baldwin, B., "The *Pseudologistes* of Lucian," *Classical Review* 12, 1962, pp. 2-5.

Baldwin 1967 = Baldwin, B., "Cover Names and Dead Victims in Juvenal," *Athenaeum* 45, 1967, pp. 304-12.

Baldwin 1969 = Baldwin, B., "The Authorship and Purpose of Lucian's *Demosthenis Encomium*," *Antichthon* 3, 1969, pp. 54-62.

Baldwin 1970 = Baldwin, B., "Hadrian's Farewell to Life: Some Arguments for Authenticity," *Classical Quarterly* 20, 1970, pp. 372-74.

Barker =   Barker, G. L. *The Historian Ephoros*, Cambridge, 1935.

                            Barnes, T. D., "Hadrian's Farewell to Life," *Classical Quarterly* 18, 1968, pp. 384-86.

Bauer =   Bauer, A., *Lukians Demosthenis Encomium*, Würzburg, 1914.

Behr =   Behr, C. A., *Aelius Aristides and the Sacred Tales*, Chicago, 1968.

                            Bellinger, A., "Lucian's Dramatic Technique," *Yale Classical Studies* 1, 1928, pp. 3-40.

Bernays =   Bernays, R., *Lukian und die Kyniker*, Berlin, 1879.

Betz =   Betz, H., *Lukian von Samosata und Das Neue Testament* Berlin, 1961.

Birley =   Birley, A. R., *Marcus Aurelius*, London, 1966.

Bompaire =   Bompaire, J., *Lucien Ecrivain*, Paris, 1958.

Bonner =   Bonner, S. F., *Dionysius of Halicarnassus*, Cambridge, 1939.

Boulanger =   Boulanger, A., *Aelius Aristide et la Sophistique*, Paris, 1923.

Boulanger, "Lucien" =   Boulanger, A., "Lucien et Aelius Aristide," *Revue de Philologie* 47, 1923, pp. 144-51.

Bouquiaux-Simon =   Bouquiaux-Simon, O., *Les Lectures Homériques de Lucien*, Brussels, 1965.

Bowersock, *Augustus* =   Bowersock, G. W., *Augustus and the Greek World*, Oxford, 1965.

Bowersock, *Sophists* =   Bowersock, G. W., *Greek Sophists in the Roman Empire*, Oxford, 1969.

Bowie =   Bowie, E. L., "Greeks and Their Past in the Second Sophistic," *Past and Present* 46, 1970, pp. 3-41.

Brock =   Brock, M. D., *Studies in Fronto and his Age*, Cambridge, 1911.

                            Brozec, M., "De Calliae Tragoedia Grammatica," *Bulletin of the Polish Academy at Cracovia*, 1938, pp. 111-14.

Caster, *Lucien* =   Caster, M., *Lucien et la Pensée Réligieuse de son temps*, Paris, 1937.

Caster, *Etudes* =   Caster, M., *Etudes sur Alexandre ou le Faux Prophète de Lucien*, Paris, 1938.

Chabert =   Chabert, *L'atticisme de Lucien*, Paris, 1897.

Chadwick =   Chadwick, H., *Origen, Contra Celsum*, Cambridge, 1953.

                            Chapman, J. J., *Lucian, Plato and Greek Morals*, Oxford, 1931.

                            Copeman, W. S. C., *A Short History of the Gout*,

Berkely, 1964.

Craig, H., "Dryden's Lucian," *Classical Philology* 16, 1921, pp. 141-63.

Croiset, *Lucien* = Croiset, M., *Essai sur la Vie et les Oeuvres de Lucien*, Paris, 1882.

Croiset, *Histoire* = Croiset, M., *Histoire de la Littérature Grècque*, Paris, 1909.

Crosby, H., "Lucian and the Art of Medicine," *Transactions of the American Philological Association* 54, 1923, pp. 15-16.

Day, J., *An Economic History of Athens under Roman Domination*, New York, 1942.

Deferrari = Deferrari, R. J., *Lucian's Atticism: The Morphology of the Verb*, Princeton, 1916.

Den Boer, W., "Religion and Literature in Hadrian's Policy," *Mnemosyne* 8, 1955, pp. 123-44.

Dittenberger, W., "Athenaeus und Sein Werk," *Apophoreton*, 1903, pp. 1-28.

Douglas = Douglas, A. E., "Cicero, Quintilian, and the Canon of Ten Attic Orators," *Mnemosyne* 9, 1956, pp. 30-40.

Dryden = Dryden, J., *Life of Lucian*, 1696. (Volume XVIII of *The Works of John Dryden*, ed. Walter Scott, London, 1808.)

Dudley = Dudley, D. R., *A History of Cynicism*, Cambridge, 1937.

Elton = Elton, G. R., *The Practice of History*, London, 1969.

Farquharson = Farquharson, A. S. L., *The Meditations of Marcus Aurelius*, Oxford, 1944.

Festa, N., "A proposito di criteri per stabilire l'autenticità degli scritti compresi nel *Corpus Lucianeum*," *Mélanges Bidez* I, 1934, pp. 377-95.

Förster = Förster, R., *Lukian in der Renaissance*, Kiel, 1886.

Frend = Frend, W. H. C., *Martyrdom and Persecution in the Early Church*, Oxford, 1965.

Gilliam, J. F., "The Plague under Marcus Aurelius," *American Journal of Philology* 82, 1961, pp. 225-51.

Goggin, M. C., "Prose Rhythm in Favorinus," *Yale Classical Studies* 12, 1951, pp. 149-201.

Graindor = Graindor, P., *Un Milliardaire antique: Hérode Atticus et sa famille*, Cairo, 1930.

Groningen, B. A. Van, "General Literary Tendencies in the Second Century A.D.," *Mnemosyne* 18,

	1965, pp. 41-56.
Grube =	Grube, G. M. A., *The Greek and Roman Critics*, London, 1965.
Hall =	Hall, F. W., *Companion to Classical Studies*, Oxford, 1913.
	Harrer, G. A., "Was Arrian Governor of Syria?," *Classical Philology* 11, 1916, pp. 338-39.
Helm, *Lucien u. Menipp* =	Helm, R., *Lucian und Menipp*, Leipzig, 1906.
Helm, *Schol. Font.* =	Helm, R., *De Luciani scholiorum fontibus*, Marburg, 1908.
Herbst =	Herbst, W., *Galeni Pergameni De Atticissantium Studiis Testimonia*, Leipzig, 1911.
	Hewitt, J. W., "A Second Century Voltaire," *Classical Journal* 20, 1924, pp. 132-42.
	Highet, G., *Juvenal the Satirist*, Oxford, 1954.
Highet, *Satire* =	Highet, G., *The Anatomy of Satire*, Princeton, 1962.
Hime =	Hime, W. L., *Lucian, the Syrian Satirist*, London, 1900.
Hitti =	Hitti, P. K., *History of Syria*, New York, 1950.
Homeyer =	Homeyer, H., *Lukian: Wie Man Geschichte Schreiben Soll*, München, 1965.
	Hook, La Rue Van, "The Literary Criticism in the *Bibliotheca* of Photius," *Classical Philology* 4, 1909, pp. 178-89.
Householder =	Householder, F. W., *Literary Quotation and Allusion in Lucian*, New York, 1941.
	Householder, F. W., "Mock Decrees in Lucian," *Transactions of the American Philological Association* 71, 1940, pp. 199-216.
	Jacoby, F., "Γενέσια: a Forgotten Festival of the Dead," *Classical Quarterly* 38, 1944, pp. 65-75.
Jones =	Jones, C. P., *Plutarch and Rome*, Oxford, 1971.
Keim =	Keim, T., *Celsus' Wahres Wort*, Zürich, 1873.
Kokolakis, *Pantomimus* =	Kokolakis, M., *Pantomimus and the Treatise* Περὶ ὀρχήσεως, Athens, 1959.
Kokolakis, *Lucian* =	Kokolakis, M., *Lucian and the Tragic Performances in His Time*, Athens, 1961.
Kougeas =	Kougeas, S. G., Ὁ Καισαρείας Ἀρέθας καὶ τὸ ἔργον αὐτοῦ, Athens, 1913.
	Kustas, G. L., "The Literary Criticism of Photius," *Hellenika* 17, 1962, pp. 132-69.
	Latte, K., "Zur Zeitbestimmung des *Antiattikista*," *Hermes* 50, 1915, pp. 373-94.
Lenz =	Lenz, F., *The Aristeides Prolegomena*, Leiden, 1959.

Lesky, A., *A History of Greek Literature*, London, 1966.

Licht, H., *Sexual Life in Ancient Greece*, London, 1932.

Lindemann =   Lindemann, H., *De Dialecto ionica recentiore*, Kiel, 1889.

Macarthy, B. P., "Lucian and Menippus," *Yale Classical Studies* 4, 1934, pp. 3-58.

Macleod =   Macleod, M. D., "Ἄν with the Future in Lucian and the *Solecist*," *Classical Quarterly* 6, 1956, pp. 102-11.

MacMullen =   MacMullen, R., *Enemies of the Roman Order*, Harvard, 1966.

Mensching =   Mensching, E., *Favorin Von Arelate*, Berlin, 1963.

Méridier =   Méridier, L., "Un lieu commun de la IIe Sophistique," *Revue de Philologie* 19, 1906, pp. 207-9.

Mesk, J., "Des Aelius Aristides verlorene Rede gegen die Tanzer," *Wiener Studien* 30, 1908, pp. 59-74.

Miller, C. W. E., "Τὸ δέ in Lucian," *Transactions of the American Philological Association* 42, 1911, pp. 131-45.

Misch =   Misch, G., *A History of Autobiography in Antiquity* (transl. into English), London, 1950.

Momigliano =   Momigliano, A., *The Development of Greek Biography*, Harvard, 1971.

Nilén, N., "Excerpta Lucianea," *Symbolae Osloenses*, 1925, pp. 26-36.

Nissen, H., "Ueber die Abfassungszeit von Arrians Anabasis," *Rheinisches Museum* 43, 1888, pp. 236-57.

Oliver =   Oliver, J. H., *The Ruling Power*, Princeton, 1953.

Pease, A. S., "Things without Honor," *Classical Philology* 21, 1926, pp. 27-42.

Peretti =   Peretti, A., *Luciano: Un intellettuale greco contro Roma*, Florence, 1946.

Pflaum, H.-G., "Lucien de Samosate, *Archistator praefecti Aegypti*," *Mélanges de l'école française de Rome* 71, 1959, pp. 281-86.

Putnam, E. J., "Lucian the Sophist," *Classical Philology* 4, 1909, pp. 162-77.

Rabe, H., "Die Ueberlieferung des Lukianscholia," *Nachrichten von der Gesellschaft der Wissenschaften zu Göttingen*, 1902, pp. 718-36.

Rabe, H., "Die Lukianstudien des Arethas," *ibid.*, 1903, pp. 643-56.

Ranke =   Ranke, E., *Pollux et Lucianus*, Quedlinberg, 1831.
Reardon =   Reardon, B. P., *Lucian: Selected Works*, New York,
                            1965.
                            Reardon, B. P., "The Greek Novel," *Phoenix* 23,
                            1969, pp. 291-309.
                            Reinmuth, O. W., "A Working List of the Prefects of
                            Egypt 30 B.C. − A.D. 299," *Bulletin of the
                            American Society of Papyrologists* 4, 1967, pp.
                            75-128.
                            Reitz, C. C., *Lexicon Lucianeum*, Utrecht, 1746.
                            Révay, J., "Un ouvrage perdu de Fronton," *Acta
                            Academiae Hungaricae*, 1951, pp. 161-90 (in
                            Russian, with a résumé in French).
                            Rigault, H., *Luciani Samosatensis quae fuerit de re
                            litteraria iudicandi ratio*, Paris, 1856.
                            Robertson, D. S., "The Authenticity and Date of
                            Lucian's *De Saltatione*," *Essays and Studies
                            Presented to William Ridgeway*, London, 1913,
                            pp. 180-85.
                            Rohde, E., "Γέγονε in den Biographica des Suidas,"
                            Rheinisches Museum 33, 1878, pp. 161 ff., 638
                            ff.
                            Rollestone, J. D., "Lucian and Medicine," *Janus* 20,
                            1915, pp. 86-108.
Rostovtzeff, *SEHRE* =   Rostovtzeff, M., *Social and Economic History of the
                            Roman Empire*, Oxford, 1957 (edition by P. M.
                            Fraser).
Rudd =   Rudd, N., *The Satires of Horace*, Cambridge, 1966.
Rutherford =   Rutherford, W. G., *The New Phrynichus*, London,
                            1881.
Sarton =   Sarton, G., *Galen of Pergamum*, Kansas, 1954.
                            Scarborough, J., *Roman Medicine*, London, 1969.
Schwartz =   Schwartz, J., *Biographie de Lucien de Samosate*,
                            Brussels, 1965.
                            Scott, K., "Humour at the Expense of the Ruler
                            Cult," *Classical Philology* 27, 1932, pp. 317-28.
Sherwin-White =   Sherwin-White, A. N., *Racial Prejudice in Imperial
                            Rome*, Cambridge, 1967.
                            Shewring, W. H., "Platonic Influence in Lucian's
                            Clausulae," *Berliner Philologische Wochenschrift*
                            28, 1934, pp. 814-16.
                            Sims, B. J., "Final Clauses in Lucian," *Classical
                            Quarterly* 2, 1952, pp. 63-73.
                            Stanton, G. R., "Marcus Aurelius, Emperor and Philo-
                            sopher," *Historia* 18, 1969, pp. 570-87.

Stark =   Stark, F., *Rome on the Euphrates*, London, 1966.
Stengel =   Stengel, A., *De Luciani Veris Historiis*, Berlin, 1911.
Stuart =   Stuart, D. R., *Epochs of Greek and Roman Bio-
                     graphy*, Berkeley, 1928.
Syme, *Ammianus* =   Syme, R., *Ammianus and the Historia Augusta*,
                     Oxford, 1968.
Syme, *Emperors* =   Syme, R., *Emperors and Biography*, Oxford, 1971.
Tackaberry =   Tackaberry, W. H., *Lucian's Relation to Plato and the
                     Post-Aristotelian Philosophers*, Toronto, 1930.
Thompson =   Thompson, C. R., *The Translations of Lucian by
                     Erasmus and St. Thomas More*, Ithaca, N.Y.,
                     1940.
                     Tondriau, J., "L'avis de Lucien sur la divinisation des
                     hommes," *Museum Helveticum* 5, 1948, pp.
                     124-32.
Turner =   Turner, P., *Lucian: Satirical Sketches*, London, 1961.
                     Varcl, L., "Verfassersverantwortlichkeit bei Juvenal
                     und Lukian," *GERAS: Studies Presented to
                     George Thomson*, Prague, 1963, pp. 225-34.
                     Wace, H., and Smith, W., *A Dictionary of Christian
                     Biography*, London, 1882.
Walbank =   Walbank, F. W., *A Historical Commentary on
                     Polybius*, Vol. I, Oxford, 1957.
Walzer =   Walzer, R., *Galen on Jews and Christians*, Oxford,
                     1949.
Wehrli =   Wehrli, F., *Die Geschichtschreibung im Lichte der
                     Antiken Theorie*, Zürich, 1947.
Winter =   Winter, R., *De Luciani scholiis quaestiones selectae*,
                     Leipzig, 1908.
                     Wilamowitz-Moellendorff, U. Von, "Asianismus und
                     Attizismus," *Hermes* 35, 1900, pp. 1-52.
                     Witke, E. C., "Marcus Aurelius and Mandragora,"
                     Classical Philology 60, 1965, pp. 23-24.
                     Wittek, M., "Liste des manuscrits de Lucien," *Scrip-
                     torium* 6, 1952, pp. 309-23.
Young =   Young, W., *Eros Denied*, New York, 1964.

Studies in Lucian

Introduction

This book begins with an analysis of the internal and external evidence for Lucian's life and career. Then comes speculation on the identities of his more important friends and enemies. This leads naturally into a detailed examination of his critical opinions on the major literary productions and issues of his age: sophistic oratory, linguistic archaism, and historiography. From here, it is no great step to the concluding themes of Lucian's attitude towards Rome and his comments on the social issues of the second century, his views on philosophy and religion, and his later reputation as the Anti-Christ.

One axe has been ground with enthusiasm. Lucian's satire was written within a series of conventions, but is almost always relevant to his own time. I have included a good deal of comparative material from Athenaeus, Aulus Gellius, Fronto, Galen, Marcus Aurelius, Phrynichus, and Philostratus' *Lives of the Sophists*. My conclusion is that we need hardly ever look outside the second century for the immediate and personal sources of Lucian's inspiration. It is obvious that he was steeped in the Greek classics, but his material is adapted to the fashions and living issues of his age.

All this is at odds with certain earlier, influential books on Lucian. Which is not to claim that these are without value and now quite superseded. Helm's *Lucian und Menipp*, for instance, is full of timeless and valuable material — especially when he is not talking about Lucian. Above all, there is Bompaire's *Lucien Ecrivain*. It will be seen that I reject his *Mimesis* approach, about

3

which a word should here be said. That Bompaire's brobding-
nagian volume is an indispensable aid to Lucianic research is
beyond dispute. But to Bompaire, Lucian's use of the Greek
cultural heritage is a literary end in itself, whereas I see it as a set
of conventions which Lucian used to relate his animadversions to
contemporary issues and targets. It will not do, for instance, to
write off the *De Historia conscribenda* as "un pastiche amusant de
Thucydide"; Lucian's pamphlet can only be appreciated within
the historiographical panorama of the first and second centuries,
and within the context of the careers of the historians or
sophist-historians, their attitudes to the Roman empire, and
relationships with generals and emperors. Since the publication of
Bompaire's book, valuable work on these latter aspects has been
done by Bowersock, Bowie, and C. P. Jones; their conclusions
have often inspired and supported my own, and their work has
illuminated the living background to Lucian's writings which
Bompaire played down or ignored.

Although I have expressed sharp disagreement with the views
of Bompaire, Helm, and others on various occasions, I have wasted
no space in elaborate attacks on any scholar living or dead. Some
of the issues involved are almost intractable, and I am no more
likely to be right or wrong than any other writer. Lucian, of
course, would not have been so temperate!

No effort has been made to provide a detailed analysis of every
piece in the Lucianic corpus. Lucian was a versatile writer, but
sometimes a tedious one (*experto crede!*); some of his exercises
are frankly not worth reading. The question of authenticity
frequently arises, but I have restricted my interest to those pieces
which play a relevant role in my arguments. Thus, the *Demosthenis Encomium* (the authenticity of which I have defended
elsewhere) is included, whereas the familiar problems of, for
example, the *Asinus*, are neglected or relegated to footnotes.
Debates over authenticity usually begin and end in personal bias
for or against the merits of the piece in question. Linguistic
statistics on one side can generally be countered by rival sets, and I
do not (yet) believe in the *deus in machina* of those who use
computers. Internal evidence would lead me to support the
rejection of the *Cynicus* and the *Philopatris*, whereas I would

return an open verdict on, say, the *Ocypus* and the *Epigrams*. Beyond this, I do not see that we can reasonably go.

Other austerities may strike the reader. I have not played the usual game of assembling chronological charts for the composition of Lucian's pieces. Since there is very rarely any positive clue, such efforts are nugatory. I have done my share of speculation, but prefer to present possibilities, not frail dogmas.

I have consistently refrained from any lengthy literary criticism, favourable or unfavourable, of Lucian. Likes and dislikes are personal matters, and the matter is perhaps the reader's privilege rather than the author's duty. I have, of course, expressed some opinions, but have played the role of analyst over that of missionary.

Lucian's works have usually been cited by the standard Latin titles, but I have elected to use English ones where these are more evocative and no more cumbersome. The inconsistency will not baffle anyone, and it would be a pity to conceal the *Dialogues of the Courtesans* or the *Octogenarians* from the eyes of the elusive general reader (if there is any such creature).

I have used the Teubner edition of C. Jacobitz (1836-41); Volume Four contains scholia, an *index nominum*, and a Greek index. This is supplemented by Nilén's Prolegomena and text (as far as it goes), and by the Loeb text of Harmon, Kilburn, and Macleod. The projected Oxford Text by Macleod is much looked forward to, but was not, of course, available during the preparation of this book. Rabe's *Scholia in Lucianum* (Teubner, 1906) is the best edition of these strange manifestations of the Byzantine mind. Other valuable work on the text was done by Fritzsche and Sommerbrodt, but was unfinished in both cases. The old Bipontine edition of Hemsterhuys and Reitz is not always to be scorned, and Reitz' *Index Lucianeus* has its uses.

The bibliography takes account of books and articles up to November 1972, by which time I had completed my manuscript and revisions. It is restricted to works cited by myself, and can, of course, be supplemented by the usual reference sources and by the extensive bibliographies (general and specialised) of Avenarius, Betz, Bompaire, and Homeyer. There is also much of relevance and value in the bibliographies of Bowersock's *Augustus and the*

Greek World and *Greek Sophists in the Roman Empire*. I claim neither to have read everything ever published on Lucian, nor to know about the existence of every article or review.

One
The Career of Lucian

Λουκιανός, Σαμοσατεύς, ὁ ἐπικληθεὶς βλάσφημος ἢ δύσφημος, ἢ ἄθεος εἰπεῖν μᾶλλον, ὅτι ἐν τοῖς διαλόγοις αὐτοῦ γελοῖα εἶναι καὶ τὰ περὶ τῶν θείων εἰρημένα παρατίθεται. γέγονε δὲ ἐπὶ τοῦ Καίσαρος Τραιανοῦ καὶ ἐπέκεινα. ἦν δὲ οὗτος τοπρὶν δικηγόρος ἐν Ἀντιοχείᾳ τῆς Συρίας, δυσπραγήσας δ' ἐν τούτῳ ἐπὶ τὸ λογογραφεῖν ἐτράπη καὶ γέγραπται αὐτῷ ἄπειρα. τελευτῆσαι δὲ αὐτὸν λόγος ὑπὸ κυνῶν, ἐπεὶ κατὰ τῆς ἀληθείας ἐλύττησεν· εἰς γὰρ τὸν Περεγρίνου βίον καθάπτεται τοῦ Χριστιανισμοῦ, καὶ αὐτὸν βλασφημεῖ τὸν Χριστὸν ὁ παμμίαρος. διὸ καὶ τῆς λύττης ποινὰς ἀρκούσας ἐν τῷ παρόντι δέδωκεν, ἐν δὲ τῷ μέλλοντι κληρονόμος τοῦ αἰωνίου πυρὸς μετὰ τοῦ Σατανᾶ γενήσεται.

This piece of pious malice from Suidas is the chief external witness to Lucian's existence. It is eked out by scrappy and uninformative *testimonia* in Lactantius, Eunapius, Isidore of Pelusium, Photius, Arethas and the scholiasts. Philostratus, perhaps rightly, omitted the satirist from his *Lives of the Sophists*. G. W. Bowersock[1] was almost justified in commenting: "Outside Lucian's own works and a wretched derivative notice in a Byzantine lexicon, there is no evidence for Lucian's existence at all."

Derived from what? The item is marked in Adler's edition as emanating from Hesychius of Miletus, whose *Pinax* is the admitted source of Suidas' implausible biographies. But Suidas inferred from the absence of Christian teachers from the *Pinax* that its

---

1. Bowersock, *Sophists*, p. 114.

compiler was not a Christian but "a man full of Hellenic drivel."[2] This excludes Hesychius as the source of the Suidas item; the language is actually much more redolent of Arethas and the scholiasts who were the real creators of Lucian the Anti-Christ.[3]

This myth had a long innings. The obloquy heaped on Erasmus for his translations of and sympathy for the satirist by such critics as Luther and the elder Scaliger is familiar.[4] As late as September 3, 1766, the *Lyceum und Gymnasium Societatis Jesu* at Regenspurg presented a drama in three acts (with musical interludes) entitled *Lucianus Samosatenus Infelix Atheus*.[5] Lucian appears in Alexandria, promoted to the rank of *Praefectus Aegypti* under Marcus Aurelius; he eventually and inevitably expires *misera morte*, in spite (or because) of being blessed by a son, Caius Lucius, who is a crypto-Christian. This son is elsewhere embellished by another engaging fiction; Dryden[6] confidently perpetuated the notion that Lucian junior survived long enough to become an intimate of the emperor Julian. It is piquant, in this hag-ridden atmosphere, to find Dr. Johnson prescribing Lucian (for his style, if not his content), to his Edial schoolboys.[7]

Back to Suidas. Deduct the abuse, and the "biography" is as

2. Suidas, s.v. Ἡσύχιος: Ἡσύχιος Μιλήσιος, υἱὸς Ἡσυχίου δικηγόρου καὶ φιλοσοφίας, γεγονὼς ἐπὶ Ἀναστασίου βασιλέως. ἔγραφεν Ὀνοματολόγον ἢ Πίνακα τῶν ἐν παιδείᾳ ὀνομαστῶν, οὗ ἐπιτομή ἐστι τοῦτο τὸ βιβλίον· καὶ Χρονικὴν ἱστορίαν, ἥντινα διεῖλεν εἰς ϛʹ διαστήματα· οὕτω γὰρ καλεῖ ἕκαστον βιβλίον· ἐν οἷς ἐμφέρονται αἱ κατὰ καιροὺς πράξεις τῶν Ῥωμαίων βασιλέων καὶ αἱ δυναστεῖαι τῶν κατὰ ἔθνος κρατησάντων τυράννων καὶ τὰ κατὰ τὸ Βυζάντιον πραχθέντα ἕως τῆς βασιλείας Ἀναστασίου τοῦ ἐπονομαζομένου Δικόρου. εἰς δὲ τὸν Πίνακα τῶν ἐν παιδείᾳ λαμμάντων ἐκκλησιαστικῶν διδασκάλων οὐδενὸς μνημονεύει· ὡς ἐκ τούτου ὑπόνοιαν παρέχειν μὴ εἶναι αὐτὸν Χριστιανόν, ἀλλὰ τῆς Ἑλληνικῆς ματαιοπονίας ἀνάπλεων.

3. This argument is documented and developed later.

4. See Thompson, pp. 44-5.

5. *Res Scenicae Ratisbonae 1740-69* (Vol. III); I came across this by chance in the British Museum in 1969.

6. Dryden, pp. 56-82. Dryden wrote this *Life of Lucian* for the *Variorum* translation of Lucian which appeared in 1711, eleven years behind schedule. See also Hardin Craig, "Dryden's Lucian," *CP*, 16, 1921, pp. 141-63. There is an obvious confusion with the Sophist Lucian addressed by Julian in *Ep.* 64.

7. *Boswell's Life of Johnson*, Oxford, 1953, p. 72.

insubstantial as the faded Helen in the *Dialogues of the Dead*. To be on the menu of dogs is no unique fate in an ancient biography; it was shared at least by Euripides and Heracleitus,[8] and someone may have had Jezebel in mind when deciding on a suitable end for the supposed blasphemer. A moot point, of course, whether this mode of death is worse than to be taken off by the gout, which was Dryden's theory.[9]

Failure at the bar in Antioch is not totally impossible. Lucian's early professional years would most likely have been spent in Antioch and Tarsus. He certainly abandoned forensic rhetoric around the age of 40, and his own high-minded explanation[10] need not be taken absolutely at face value. Lucian was as dedicated to fame and fortune as any orthodox sophist. The author of the *Nigrinus*, the *Demonax*, and the *De Mercede Conductis* was not ashamed to remind audiences that he won reputation and wealth in Gaul,[11] or that he was on friendly terms with the governor of Cappadocia;[12] his translation to the imperial service in Egypt is the

8. For Euripides see Aulus Gellius, *NA* 15.20; Athenaeus, *Deipnoso-phistae*, 13.597. Diogenes Laertius has the Heracleitus version from Neanthes. For the currency of such fables see *Boswell's Life of Johnson*, p. 525: "The custom of eating dogs at Otaheite being mentioned, Goldsmith observed, that this was also a custom in China; that a dog-butcher is as common there as any other butcher; and that when he walks abroad all the dogs fall on him. JOHNSON. 'That is not owing to his killing dogs, Sir. I remember a butcher at Lichfield, whom a dog that was in the house where I lived, always attacked. It is the smell of carnage which provokes this, let the animals he has killed be what they may.'" See also Stuart, pp. 146-7.

9. Dryden, p. 61. Gout is an old inference from the *Tragodopodagra* and *Ocypus*. *Heracles* 7 refers to Lucian's old age and disabilities of foot, but gout is not specifically mentioned. Gout is classified as a disease of the wealthy in *Menippus* 11, *Saturnalia* 28; the malady is apostrophised in *Epigram* 47. Fronto suffered from gout, as perhaps did Aulus Gellius who had the hopeful notion from Theophrastus (*NA* 4.13) that it could be relieved by soothing flute melodies. But the logical place for Lucian's gout is in a footnote.

10. *Bis Accusatus* 32, *Piscator* 25; but see the next note.

11. *Bis Accusatus* 27, *Apology* 15. In both cases Lucian stresses wealth over fame.

12. *Alexander* 55. The governor lent him an armed guard for use against the prophet. This official might have enjoyed *Epigram* 43, which ridicules Cappadocian orators.

ultimate comment. The fact that success came in Gaul, well outside the main centres of sophistic activity, may indicate that he found little room at the top in the professionally crowded centres of the East, and so opted for the status of big fish in a smaller pond, which he hoped would be temporary. On the other hand, Lucian had his fair share of malice when things did not go his way; I doubt that he would have published his compliment to the acumen of Antiochenes,[13] for all his Syrian affections, had he shared the opinions of the emperors Hadrian and Julian on the inhabitants of that frivolous metropolis.[14]

The lone chronological reference in Suidas is perplexingly vague. Lucian's birth is usually assigned to 117 or thereabouts, with varying degrees of misplaced confidence.[15] But if γέγονε means "flourished,"[16] his birth should be pushed back rather than forwards. 117 has a perverse attraction in that it produced the suffering and insufferable Aelius Aristides,[17] but nothing should be made of the coincidence. The matter may be complicated by an apparent reference in the *Eunuchus* to Favorinus: τις Ἀκαδημαϊκὸς εὐνοῦχος ἐκ Κελτῶν ὀλίγον πρὸ ἡμῶν εὐδοκιμήσας ἐν τοῖς Ἕλλησιν.[18] Favorinus is datable to the period 80-150,[19] and Suidas' chronology is striking: γεγονὼς ἐπὶ Τραιανοῦ τοῦ Καίσαρος καὶ παρατείνας μέχρι τῶν Ἀδριανοῦ χρόνων τοῦ βασιλέως. The *Eunuchus* is a satire on the competition for one of the chairs of philosophy established at Athens by Marcus Aurelius,

---

13. *De Saltatione* 76.

14. For Hadrian's hatred of Antioch see *HA, Hadrian* 14.1; for Julian, of course, the *Misopogon*.

15. The most fanciful are Schwartz, Bouquiaux-Simon; Bompaire on Lucian's actual career. Croiset, *Lucien* is still worth reading. The article in *RE* XIII.2 197, s.v. *Lukianos*, is by R. Helm. Sobriety and speculation are adroitly mingled in Allinson, *Lucian*. Hime is almost worthless. The reconstructions of Lucian's early career by Householder are implausible but entertaining. See also E. J. Putnam, "Lucian the Sophist," *CP* 4, 1909, pp. 162-77. More recent and cautious is Reardon.

16. See the classic study by E. Rohde, "Γέγονε in den Biographica des Suidas," *Rheinisches Museum* 33, 1878, pp. 161 ff., 638 ff.

17. See Schwartz, p. 9 and Boulanger.

18. *Eunuchus* 7. In *Adversus Indoctum* 20, the false Nero of the late first century is vaguely dated κατὰ τοὺς προπάτορας ἡμῶν.

19. The *testimonia* are assembled in Mensching, pp. 3-7.

and cannot have been written before the late 170s.[20] Lucian would have been at least 30 before Favorinus, whom he probably did not like,[21] died; to describe him as living a little before his own time is peculiar if the traditional chronology is right.

This is a minor puzzle (it could be explained on the simple assumption that Lycinus is given the comment for dramatic purposes only, and the allusion might not even be to Favorinus,[22] but it serves to point up the frailty of modern attempts to fabricate elaborate chronological tables for Lucian's works. The latter furnish very few clues. It is certain that Lucian survived Marcus Aurelius;[23] he was exactly 40 when he published the *Hermotimus*, but there is no way of expiscating a precise date for this piece;[24] he lived long enough to call himself an old man on at least three separate occasions, though his language varies and perhaps some concession to the fashionable hypochondria of the age has to be made;[25] he claims to have been very old when appointed to his position in Egypt, but can still look forward to the prospect of higher things in the future.[26]

20. See A. H. Harmon in the Loeb *Lucian*, Vol. 5, 1936, p. 329.

21. In *Demonax* 12 and 13, there are two thrusts against Favorinus by Demonax, including the inevitable eunuch joke. Bowersock, *Sophists*, (p. 116) is wrong in saying that Herodes is the only major sophist mentioned by Lucian. It is notable that both Favorinus and Peregrinus are respected by Aulus Gellius but mocked by Lucian.

22. I think it probably is a genuine allusion; it should be noted that the real reading is ἐκ Κελτῶν, although Harmon printed the marginal Πελασγῶν τελῶν. In *Alexander* 27, Severianus is dubbed "a foolish Celt"; but see Bowersock, *Sophists*, (p. 87) for Lucian's loose use of the term.

23. *Alexander* 48.

24. *Hermotimus* 13; the age coincides with *Bis Accusatus* 32 where Lucian describes his "conversion" to philosophy. Schwartz and Bouquiaux-Simon assign the *Hermotimus* to 165; this could be about right, but all such dates rest upon the hypothetical year of Lucian's birth. Perhaps we should not even take the age of 40 as literal truth; Marcus Aurelius (*Meditations* 11.1) gives 40 as the ideal age of reason in a man.

25. *Heracles* 7-8; *Apology* 4 (ἐν γήρᾳ δὲ ὑστάτῳ); *Pro Lapsu* 1 (πρεσβύτης ἀνήρ). See Bowersock, *Sophists*, (pp. 71-5), for the hypochondria manifest in Fronto's correspondence, Aelius Aristides, and the popular interest in Galen's anatomical displays.

26. *Apology* 12; he claims to look forward to a governorship.

I analyse the internal evidence for Lucian's career in the light of Bowersock's provocative statement: "There is indeed nothing to suggest that he ever ranked (or practised) as a sophist." The comment has already attracted an exclamation from one reviewer,[27] but the suggestion is at least valid; I suspect Philostratus would have nodded agreement.

Lucian was born in Samosata in the old kingdom of Commagene. It is now the pathetic village of Samsat or Sumaysat,[28] but was a city of some strategic consequence in the last years of Trajan. Householder[29] proposed that Lucian might have had Roman citizenship through his father who could have come to Samosata with the *Legio XVI Flavia*; there is no point in arguing the unarguable. Lucian only mentions his home town once by name, and then in a humorous context;[30] it played no part in his occasional generalised nostalgia for Syria. He does not trouble to flatter its citizens in his vaguely autobiographic *Somnium*, and there is nothing to suggest that he spent any money there on the traditional sophistic benefactions for public buildings and private ego.

The family was not well off, though able to afford to send the young Lucian to school. We can take this at face value, unlike some of his reminiscences which owe more to art than life.[31] It was unusual for a sophist to come from a poor or obscure family (Lucian's parents were trying to bask in the reflected local glory of his sculptor-uncle); the rags-to-riches saga of a Trimalchio was out of fashion, and Lucian's gibes at the humble origins of his victim in the *Rhetorum Praeceptor* were as sure of a laugh as had been

27. B. P. Reardon, *CW* 63, 1970, p. 207.
28. See, e.g., Hitti, *passim*; Stark, *passim*.
29. Householder, pp. 94 ff.
30. *De Historia conscribenda* 24; one of the hopeful compilers of *Parthica* misplaced Samosata into Mesopotamia. Lucian does not seem much perturbed by the error.
31. Such as the ophthalmia which took him to Rome and the intellectual eye-opening by Nigrinus. Turner, p. 8, would even relate his boyish enthusiasm for modelling to reminiscence of Aristophanes, which is perhaps too sceptical. However, the point is that one can never be quite sure with Lucian.

those of Demosthenes against Aeschines.[32]

Parents were important to a sophist when the profession ran in the family, though the homage of a Galen to his father is neatly balanced by Avidius Cassius (son of the Syrian Avidius Heliodorus) who let the side down by rebelling against Marcus Aurelius, thus provoking one of Herodes Atticus' most laconic utterances.[33] The overt relationship between Lucian and his parents has something in common with Horace; the mother drops out after her brother had shown himself to be an Orbilius to her son's first attempts at sculpting, the father is still alive and moved with Lucian's family to Amastris during the Alexander of Abonoteichus affair.[34] We know nothing of Lucian's wife; perhaps she learned to keep her mouth shut to avoid the charge of archaism. Had Lucian made an illustrious match, he would certainly have reminded his audiences of the fact. His attempt to dissuade Rutilianus, proconsul of Asia, from marrying Alexander's daughter Selene, over whom the governor was mooning, does not imply any feelings against matrimony.[35] The long-lived son of Dryden's imaginings is mentioned in the *Eunuchus* as being "quite young" and perhaps marked out for philosophy,[36] a hazardous career with such a father.

Lucian's painful and abortive experience as an apprentice sculptor (there is something in common here with the carpenter-

32. *Rhetorum Praeceptor* 24; the victim is mocked for his servile Egyptian origins and the customary sexual versatility by which he made his way. Jokes about Egyptian birth seem designed more for a Roman than a Greek audience; several sophists hailed from Naucratis, though Alexandria is oddly out of the main sophistic stream (see Bowersock, *Sophists*, p. 20). One wonders how tactful Lucian was in his official dealings with the natives in Egypt. The obvious comparison to Juvenal should be resisted. See *Pseudologistes* 27 and *Adversus Indoctum* 23 for similar sneers at low social status and lower behaviour. The theory that Pollux is the butt of the *Rhetorum Praeceptor* will be discussed later.

33. Philostratus, *VS*, p. 563: Ἡρώδης Κασσίῳ· ἐμάνης.

34. *Alexander* 56; the reference is to τὸν πατέρα καὶ τοὺς ἐμούς. Lucian retained a certain Xenophon in his company: Slave? Freedman? Lover?

35. *Alexander* 54.

36. *Eunuchus* 13. I suppose it is not impossible that this son is a literary figment, but scepticism must be kept within reasonable bounds.

father of Secundus of Athens) is credible and unimportant; it is naive to see this episode as directly responsible for his later interest in sculpture and painting. Unless modern psychologists are wrong (a possibility to be relished), Lucian should have been put off for life. Nor is his prophetic dream of any moment. Such visions were almost mandatory in the second century;[37] they may have boosted the sales of Artemidorus' *Oneirocritica*. In Lucian's case, *Paideia* is probably wise after the event; she merely catalogues the usual prizes of a sophistic career (wealth, fame, public office) in a seductive Madison Avenue style.

Like many documents, the *Somnium* is more significant for its omissions than its contents. It stops on the above note of conventional promise. Lucian's alleged successes in Ionia, Greece, Italy, and Gaul are proclaimed with equal vagueness in the *Bis Accusatus*.[38] His Gallic experiences also crop up in the *Heracles* and the *Apology*;[39] the *Heracles* is a "come-back" performance, the *Apology* dwells on the size of the fees he used to command. Both passages are an old man's memories which perhaps grew with the years. This is not to say that Lucian was not a fair exchange for Favorinus! However, if the *Somnium* was really the speech of the local boy returning home after making good, then Lucian (who was not afflicted by an excess of modesty) had remarkably little to boast of.

The geography of his career is pertinent. Householder toyed with the notion that Lucian's "early wanderings" in Ionia were with an itinerant patent-medicine show. A harmless delusion: his respect for the medical profession was inspired by more than this, and I am not thinking of his alleged gout and sore eyes.[40] The

---

37. See Bowersock, *Sophists*, pp. 73-4 for a documented discussion. In *Bis Accusatus* 1, Zeus complains of the work forced on the gods by the demand for dreams.

38. *Bis Accusatus* 27; no particular cities are mentioned.

39. *Heracles* 7, *Apology* 15; the references are again vague.

40. *Nigrinus* 2; the possible imagery is obvious, and may be sustained by the ocular malady of one of the characters in the *Symposium* of the aesthetically blind Lexiphanes (*Lexiphanes* 4). Still, eye disease was common enough (Fronto inevitably included it in his vast catalogue of complaints); see Scarborough.

relationship between doctors and sophists, the role of doctors in the Atticist controversies, and a possible connection between Lucian and Galen, are the cardinal factors.[41] In the *Bis Accusatus*, Oratory claims to have found the young Lucian at a loose end in Ionia, wearing a Syrian caftan and βάρβαρον ἔτι τὴν φωνήν. This phrase recurs at least four more times in Lucian, and implies either a pronounced accent or indifferent command of the niceties of Greek; it does not mean that Lucian was speaking "Syrian."[42] Accent was certainly an important issue in the Sophistic movements. Quintilian was exercised over the need to inculcate a good accent in boys;[43] Hadrian, before he became emperor, was laughed at by the Senate for his provincial intonation;[44] Galen ridicules critics who condemned errors of grammar and accent in others;[45] Herodes quashed Peregrinus for insulting him in "semi-barbarous" Greek (Lucian would have enjoyed that exchange!), and was in turn put in his place by the exotic rustic Heracles-Agathion, who was audacious enough (he was supposed to be eight feet tall, which must have boosted his confidence in debate against the great man) to tell him that his own rustic Attic was purer than the Athenian which was corrupted by foreign influences.[46]

It is again significant that Oratory glosses over Lucian's performance in Ionia and Greece;[47] Italy and Gaul give more scope for pride. The visit to Rome described in the *Nigrinus* is credible, and took place fairly early in Lucian's career; the *Pro Lapsu*, written late in his life, turns to some extent on the niceties of Latin style (Lucian includes in it perhaps his sole overt claim to know some Latin), and may also have been published in the capital; it is hard to draw the line between the acts of writing and

41. See later for an attempt to demonstrate a possible personal relationship between Lucian and Galen.

42. See *Pseudologistes* 1, *Adversus Indoctum* 4, *Vitarum Auctio* 10, *De Mercede Conductis* 24; the point is discussed by Householder, p. 95, n. 2.

43. Quintilian, 1.1.13.

44. *HA, Hadrian* 3.1: agrestius pronuntians risus esset.

45. *De Ordine Suorum Librorum* 5.

46. Philostratus, *VS*, p. 563 (Herodes and Peregrinus), p. 553 (the exchanges with Heracles-Agathion).

47. *Bis Accusatus* 27.

publication. A visit to Italy is indicated in *Herodotus* 5. The late
Heracles seems to have been delivered in Gaul (*Heracles* 7), and
there is a reference to a trip up the Po in *Electrum* 2. The
Herodotus and the *Scythian* were probably delivered in Macedonia, and the *Fugitivi* almost certainly at Philippolis in 165-166
(immediately after the death of Peregrinus); Lucian is again
observable as well off the beaten track. Antioch in the 160s was
the scene of the *Imagines* and *Pro Imaginibus*; so also of the *De
Saltatione*. All three can be connected with the emperor Verus.[48]
The *Pseudologistes* can reasonably be assigned to Ephesus.[49] The
Eunuchus has particular topical impact in Athens, as would have
the *Rhetorum Praeceptor* if we accepted the identification of
Lucian's victim with Pollux.[50] Assuming 165 to have been the year
of Peregrinus' flamboyant self-immolation, Lucian's presence at
Olympia is established for 153, 157, 161, 165.[51] The *Alexander*
refers to a journey to Amastris, and Lucian had somehow become
acquainted with the governor of Cappadocia. The *Apology* is
obviously written in Egypt, where Lucian had previously known
the *grammaticus*, Socrates of Mopsus.[52] One piece of negative

48. The *Imagines* compliment Verus' mistress Panthea, and with its
companion piece can be assigned to ca. 162-166, when Verus was in the East.
The eulogy is time-serving to a degree, but we need not be excessively
outraged. There was no reason why Lucian should not compliment a pretty
girl (though his wife may not have been so tolerant). His motives, like
Panthea herself, tend to suffer from the bad press accorded to Verus in the
HA (which dubs the girl *vulgaris amica*); but the reference to Panthea in
Marcus Aurelius (*Meditations*, 8.37) is no worse than neutral. The *De
Saltatione* is a compliment to Verus, who was notoriously keen on dancers; it
may also have been a slap at Aristides' invective against the art. The fact that
Lucian ridicules mimes in the *Pseudologistes* is no argument against the
authenticity of the *De Saltatione*; personal malice often outweighs consis-
tency. On the whole question see D. S. Robertson, "The authenticity and
date of Lucian's *De Saltatione*," in *Essays Ridgeway*, pp. 180-85, and
Kokolakis, *Pantomimus*.

49. *Pseudologistes* 10.

50. Pollux was appointed to the chair of Rhetoric at Athens by
Commodus.

51. *Peregrinus* 35.

52. *Soloecistes* 5. The authenticity of this dialogue, which I accept, will
be considered later. Both Socrates and Mopsus are shadowy; Macleod (Loeb

evidence states that Lucian never visited Libya.[53] It is obvious that he spent a good deal of time in Greece, Athens in particular, and visited Corinth at least once.[54] However, the temptation to equate a dialogue or piece set in Greece with a particular performance in a particular area should be resisted. Otherwise, the sophists with their effusions on Marathon, Demosthenes, and so on would have to be absurdly circumscribed in geographical terms.

Lucian's translation to the imperial service in Egypt is another mystery. His elevation may have been ironically appropriate to one so concerned with style (we imagine he was a meticulous drafter of documents and may have been a rare civil servant who could write an intelligible memorandum), but who was responsible for his appointment and why? His actual position may have been *archistator praefecti Aegypti*;[55] Lucian himself is quite vague on the point. Equally odd is the fact that he felt the need to justify his position in the *Apology*, since the *De Mercede Conductis* had attacked a very different class of men from civil servants, and in the *Somnium* the hope of public office is listed as one of the normal ambitions of a sophist. Schwartz[56] assumes that Lucian owed his preferment to Calvisius Statianus whose career was ruined in the aftermath of Avidius Cassius' revolt; Statianus came from Verona, and Lucian is supposed to have met him in Gaul on his youthful visit to that region. After 175, Lucian lost his position and resumed his literary career in Athens. This is pure hypothesis, as is Bouquiaux-Simon's tentative date of 186 for the death of Lucian at the age of 67.[57] I do not doubt that Lucian owed his rank to a friend in high places. In spite of his possibly

---

Lucian, Vol. 8, 1967, p. 16) is tempted to equate Socrates with Demonax, with whom Lucian was intimate for a long time (*Demonax* 1). But why would Lucian suppress the real name of a man to whom he was prepared to consecrate a eulogy? The point is immaterial if one rejects the *Soloecistes* as spurious.

53. *Dipsades* 6.

54. *De Historia conscribenda* 17.

55. See H. G. Pflaum, *Mélanges de l'Ecole française de Rome*, 71, 1959, pp. 281 ff.; Bowersock, *Sophists*, p. 114, n. 6.

56. Schwartz, pp. 12-13.

57. Bouquiaux-Simon, p. 26.

anti-Roman comments and his capacity for personal feuds, he was more inclined to speak softly of emperors and dignitaries.[58] Not for him was the temerity of Alexander "Clay-Plato" who once rebuked an emperor for inattention.[59] What exactly prompted his *Apology* is obscure; we might have made a guess had we known anything about Sabinus, the addressee of the pamphlet.[60]

I refrain from the fashionable construction of charts which purport to show the exact years and venues of particular Lucianic pieces. It will do no harm to believe that he was born late in Trajan's reign or in the early years of Hadrian, and died in the period of Commodus (we could, of course, enjoy ourselves by assuming the authenticity of the *Octogenarians* and go on to infer that the piece was partly a tribute to Lucian's own attainment of this age). References to Peregrinus, the Christians, Panthea, the Plague, the Parthian War, and Marcus Aurelius may indicate that he was particularly active in the period 161-169. It should be iterated that there is virtually nothing in the evidence, internal and external, for Lucianic chronology that deserves the status of fact.

Whether we should follow Philostratus and Bowersock in denying him the label of sophist is an open question. The so-called "conversion" of Lucian may be nothing more than a gloss to cover his abandonment of an unsuccessful career at the bar. In any event, a similar shift of emphasis is attested by Fronto and the *Meditations* for Marcus Aurelius,[61] and the supposed collapse and insanity of Hermogenes is also parallel.[62] It would be dangerous to invoke the case of Juvenal to explain Lucian,[63] or to assume that

58. Not invariably (note the cases of Favorinus and Herodes), but some adverse comments could have been safely published after the victims' deaths; the *Alexander* and *Peregrinus* prove Lucian's lack of scruple in this regard.

59. Philostratus, *VS*, p. 571.

60. Schwartz, p. 12, assumes he was a *rhetor*, without any evidence.

61. Fronto, *De eloquentia* 4: eloquentiae studium reliquisse, ad philosophiam devertisse; *Meditations*, 1.7, 1.13.

62. Philostratus quotes contemporary gibes against Hermogenes for his supposed failure of nerve, and ignores his technical writings (*VS*, p. 577); Suidas improves upon the situation by having Hermogenes go insane.

63. A good deal of ink has been spilled on the possible literary relationship between Juvenal and Lucian; see a survey and comment on much of it by Highet, p. 252. The trend continues with L. Varcl, "Verfassersverant-

satire is inevitably the product of the satirist's frustrations. A simple desire to establish a name outside the main fashions of the second century might be explanation enough. Lucian's brand of humour was not a very dangerous one; the mime Marullus went so far as to ridicule Verus and Marcus Aurelius with impunity.[64] Lucian was original in that he won no great fame in the main Eastern centres, was associated with no public benefactions, did not attract a loud following or perform before emperors,[65] and had no connections of family or marriage on which to capitalise. All of which was enough to explain his omission by Philostratus.[66] The question ultimately is hair-splitting, if not meaningless. "Sophist" was a flexible label (Lucian could apply it to Christ in the *Peregrinus*), and the distinction between orator and philosopher sometimes breaks down. The orthodoxies of the age can make Lucian seem more unusual than he really was. Whilst I have no time for the obsessional *Mimesis* of Bompaire,[67] it is obvious that Lucian worked within a well-established framework of ideas and methods. Apart from his religious satire, which (allied with his social satire) was his most heterodox achievement, his nature

wortlichkeit bei Juvenal und Lukian," *GERAS: Studies Thomson*, pp. 225-34. There is no evidence either way; the only safe comment is that Lucian would not have forgiven Juvenal for his attitude to Syrians and *Graeculi*. Lucian's anti-Roman sentiments will be considered later.

64. *HA, Marcus Antoninus* 8.1: eos Marullus, sui temporis mimographus, cavillando impune perstringeret.

65. E.g., Aristides (Philostratus, *VS*, p. 583) had the audacity (or caution) to ask Marcus Aurelius for permission to bring in his own students to cheer his performance.

66. The implications of Lucian's omission must be cautiously handled. There was a case for including Galen (who appears in Athenaeus, though to no great effect in the extant parts), but the medical man perhaps shared too many of Lucian's opinions and was too close to the technical interests of Hermogenes to win a place in the declaimers' gallery. Other signal omissions include Hegesias and Fronto. We should not reach too eagerly for the traditional lifebelt of assuming *lacunae* in the manuscripts. Inclusion or exclusion of a particular figure was quite subjective, conditioned in part by the presence of other collections of biographies. Not all of Philostratus' chosen race feature in Suidas.

67. A much better approach to the influence of literary tradition and second century practices on Lucian is Bowie, pp. 3-41.

writing consisted in isolating common tendencies of the sophistic movement within his revival of the comic dialogue and the prose lampoon (not forgetting the literary epistle). Lucianic trademarks such as ridicule of extreme archaism and the vicious personal attack are actually commonplaces of the age (the game was played from emperors downwards). The label "original" does not mean much at the best of times. Lucian was not in any real way a unique figure. The intellectual and academic (terms not always synonymous) life of the second century was far less uniform than is often supposed. Every established figure had his detractors, every coterie its rival. Lucian's decision to use the dialogue form for some (though by no means all) of his views was partly inspired by the endless real dialogues between factions and individuals (Aulus Gellius is full of dialogue scenes, and Philostratus uses personal exchanges as a major type of illustrative anecdote). Lucian stood out in one way, Hermogenes in another, Galen in many. All three suffer by omission or distortion from the biographers.

The precise details of Lucian's career are beyond retrieval; our curiosity suffers more than our comprehension of his particular role in the age. He was well aware of one deadly rule of the game: publish or perish. Indeed, this was the common attraction for sophistic practitioners. Some perished, all published.

Two
Friends and Enemies

Dio Chrysostom felt the need to apologise for and defend his allusions to Nero and other "despised moderns,"[1] and the absurd Apollonius of Tyana was upset by Greeks who were adopting Roman names.[2] Lucian himself generally styles himself "Lycinus" in his dialogues, though not invariably.[3] It is commonly claimed that his literary method precludes any great amount of contemporary allusion,[4] or that he avoids attacking the major sophists of his day.[5] The truth is that, although his references are frequently too vague for us to identify the precise object of his attack (the same is obviously true of any ancient satirist), Lucian is in no way unwilling to name names in either a friendly or hostile spirit. His range is wide: from emperors to poetasters, from imperial concubines to bawling cynics. The allusion may be a direct one from Lycinus or put into the mouth of the hero or villain of a pamphlet. Frequently the actual name is merely hinted at, or

1. *Oration* 21, 11.
2. Philostratus, *Life of Apollonius*, 4.5; he was upset by the presence of the name Fabricius in the ranks of the Ionian Greeks of Smyrna.
3. Bowie, p. 32, is slightly misleading on this. Lucian uses "Lucianus" in the initial greetings of the *Nigrinus* and *Peregrinus*; he is also Lucianus in *Alexander* 55. Lycinus is his normal name in dialogue, apart from the disputed *Soloecistes* and perhaps the *Piscator* (though in Harmon's Loeb *Lucian*, Vol. 3, 1921, he appears throughout as Parresiades). As Bowie notes, Lucian ridicules one of the writers of *Parthica* for transliterating or translating Roman names into Greek (*De Historia conscribenda* 21).
4. See especially Bompaire, pp. 471-538.
5. Bowersock, *Sophists*, p. 116.

withheld, but the audience is given enough clues to do the detective work of identification. His victims, like Horace's or Juvenal's,[6] may be alive or dead; Lucian did not subscribe to the hypocrisy of *de mortuis nil nisi bonum*. Close study of these references serves to establish his position with respect to the individuals and issues of the second century, and to rescue him from the vacuum of Bompaire's *Mimesis* and the poor man's Menippus tag fastened on him by Helm.[7]

Positive references begin at the top of the social and political tree. The deification of Marcus Aurelius and his campaigns against the Marcomanni and Quadi are mentioned once in a neutral tone. Lucian does not indulge here in any comment on the apotheosis of emperors; if he knew it, it is fairly sure that he would have relished the *bon mot* of Vespasian on the subject.[8] There is no evidence for any reason on Lucian's part to dislike Marcus; on the contrary, there was reason enough to be grateful if his Egyptian appointment fell within the 170s. The compliment to Marcus' scholarship and respect for learning in *Adversus Indoctum* 22 is hardly surprising in view of the emperor's involvement in the sophistic movements. However, this accolade is immediately balanced by an overt reference to Marcus' addiction to mandragora. The "Stoic Prince" as a "junkie" presents a piquant spectacle; the allusion was not notably tactless (Galen openly discusses the case), but Lucian does not risk any jokes on the subject.[9] Perhaps Marullus the mime was less covert. On the other side, the reference by Marcus (*Meditations*, 6.47) to "Menippus and men like him" may indicate that the emperor was familiar with Lucian's Menippus dialogues.[10]

6. On Horace see Rudd, pp. 132-59; for Juvenal see my article, (Baldwin, 1967), pp. 304-12.

7. Helm, *Lucian und Menipp*; for criticism of Helm see Barbara P. Macarthy, "Lucian and Menippus," *Yale Class Stud* 4, 1934, pp. 3-58.

8. The cults of Alexander and of Amphilochus and Trophonius are laughed at in the *Dialogues of the Dead*. See K. Scott, "Humour at the expense of the Ruler Cult," *CP* 27, 1932, pp. 317-28.

9. On the addiction of Marcus see T. W. Africa, "The opium addiction of Marcus Aurelius," *Journal of the History of Ideas* 22, 1961, pp. 97-102; E. C. Witke, "Marcus Aurelius and Mandragora," *CP* 60, 1965, pp. 23-4; Birley, pp. 295-6.

10. See the Commentary of A. S. L. Farquharson, 1944, p. 320.

Lucian's slightly ambivalent attitude to Marcus was probably less personal than ideological (their respective attitudes to philosophy need no comment); it falls far short of the frequent clashes between emperors and sophists which occasionally evoke the current atmosphere between academics and American presidents.[11]

More suggestive is the possible relationship between Lucian and Verus, adumbrated in the previous chapter. The praise of Panthea and the *De Saltatione* might have been inspired by a meeting of the satirist and the emperor. Decent caution is needed in an area where conjecture could quickly degenerate into wild fiction. Yet it is reasonable to suggest that the light-hearted Verus would have been more congenial to Lucian than Marcus, and it is not unduly cynical to believe that, with so many other sophists feathering their nests with Marcus, Lucian saw in Verus an easier road to patronage.[12] The picture of Verus as a compound of Caligula, Nero, and Commodus is strictly the invention of the *Historia Augusta*; contemporary and near contemporary accounts are sketchy but kinder.[13] The statement of the *Historia Augusta* (*Verus*, 2.6) that Verus liked philosophy (or at least his teachers), poetry, and oratory is borne out by the evidence of Fronto. Lucian's interest in the swarm of would-be chroniclers of *Parthica* assumes an extra dimension in this context. However, these speculations are healthily arrested by another claim of the *Historia Augusta* concerning Verus: risui fuit omnibus Syris (7.4).

Antoninus Pius (not actually named) is conventionally praised as gentle and tolerant, but this observation is introduced to heighten the villainy of Peregrinus, to which end Lucian would have praised virtually anybody.[14] Emperors on the whole are

11. Bowersock, *Sophists, passim*; see, e.g., the disputes between Favorinus and Hadrian, Polemo and Antoninus Pius (before the latter became emperor), Alexander "Clay-Plato" and Antoninus.

12. Though his pitch might have been queered by Fronto. It is notable that Verus is generally excluded from the accounts of Philostratus.

13. Contemporary accounts, of course, perhaps had to be kinder, but the combined weight of Marcus Aurelius, Fronto, Galen, Dio, and even Julian outweigh the *Historia Augusta*. See Birley, pp. 215-6, for a review of the evidence.

14. *Peregrinus* 18. Lucian would have appreciated Pius' sarcasm on

carefully avoided, and the fates of tyrants and kings in Lucian's
Underworld cannot be safely related to any particular *princeps*.
They are rather a matter for Lucian's social satire, an important
theme but not a dangerous one in the Antonine period and quite
compatible with support for the Principate. Our own age shows
that no branch of satire is more respectable or more easily attuned
to the current "Establishment's" own official attitudes. There was
a good deal of social unrest in the second century, and no shortage
of individuals willing to take advantage of it. Lucian had first-hand
experience of straitened circumstances, if not abject poverty, and
his sympathy for the poor was genuine (though perhaps purely
intellectual: I do not see him as a radical or a "freedom-fighter").
But expressions of sympathy for the poor came from emperors
too, and were not likely to get many writers into trouble.[15]

References to high public officials (excluding the separate case
of Herodes Atticus) are peculiar. Severianus, the "foolish Celt,"
who was defeated at Elegeia in 161, is ridiculed for trusting one of
Alexander's prophecies, but the mentions of the deceased general
in the *De Historia conscribenda* are restrained where they need not
have been.[16] P. Mummius Sisenna Rutilianus is praised as a man of
breeding and versatile competence; however, his belief in Alexander's prognostications and his marriage to the latter's daughter at
the age of sixty, against Lucian's urgings, doomed him to insanity,
death at the age of seventy, and the claim that he was a religious
maniac.[17] Lollianus Avitus owes his presence in *Alexander* 57 to
an emendation;[18] Lucian was upset by his efforts to shield
Alexander out of regard for Rutilianus.[19] However, the friendly

philosophers over-concerned with money (see Bowersock, *Sophists*, p. 34, for
the anecdote).

15. The theme is developed later. To the usual literature on the
Antonine period add G. R. Stanton, "Marcus Aurelius, Emperor and
Philosopher," *Historia* 18, 1969, pp. 570-87.

16. *De Historia conscribenda* 21, 25, 26.

17. *Alexander* 34 and *passim*; see Bowersock, *Sophists*, p. 71, for
Rutilianus.

18. By Burmeister; Avitus is exhumed from the ἄνεκτος or αὑτός of the
manuscripts.

19. *Alexander* 57.

governor of Cappadocia who provided Lucian with two soldiers as armed escort is not named. Since the bodyguard was given to Lucian as protection on his way overland to the coast, we may entertain malicious doubts about the quality of the relationship. More understandable, perhaps, is the absence of names from the *Apology* (apart from the unknown addressee, Sabinus). Few satirists, especially those who have risen in the world, advertise their gratitude. A strong impression is left that Lucian is happier naming enemies than friends in political contexts, happiest when those enemies are conveniently dead. An attitude perhaps bred of caution (one never knew when a powerful patron might fall), though any dogmatic principle should be avoided.

The authenticity of the *Octogenarians* is usually denied. Perhaps wrongly. Longevity was a topic of interest and encouragement in an age of hypochondria. Phlegon of Tralles, freedman of Hadrian, wrote on the subject,[20] and Aulus Gellius has a disquisition on the special dangers attending a man's sixty-third year.[21] Fronto defined old age as "crepusculum quod longum esse non potest."[22] If Lucian was the author, an interesting possibility emerges. The treatise is dedicated to a certain Quintillus. Could this conceal one of the brothers Quintilii who had glorious careers (consuls together in 151), were embroiled in the sophistic feuds (they had no taste for Herodes), and finally liquidated by Commodus (for which they win a generous epitaph from Dio)?[23]

From politicians to sophists is a small step, sometimes no step at all. Lucian's apparent distaste for Favorinus has already been noticed. His attitude (unless we are making too much of his amusement at Favorinus' curious anatomy) is conditioned by a general willingness to be unkind to members of the circle in which Aulus Gellius moved. Peregrinus is the other chief case in point; it will be suggested later that Fronto may also have been a target. There is nothing to sustain Allinson's idea that Lucian participated

20. See Bowie, p. 11, n. 24.
21. *NA* 15.7.
22. In a letter to Arrius Antoninus (Haines 2.186).
23. Bowersock, *Sophists*, pp. 87-8. The Quintilii feature in Philostratus, *VS*, p. 559 and p. 582; Dio Cassius, 71.33, 72.5-7; *HA*, *Commodus* 4.9.

in the donnish talk at Cephisia.²⁴ A pity; imagination could run riot if the notion were accepted. In general terms, it is not impossible that the *Convivium* was a recognisable, if unfair, skit on the high table atmosphere evoked in Gellius (perpetuated later by Athenaeus and Macrobius). The bibliomane butt of the *Adversus Indoctum* and the sesquipedalian victim in the *Lexiphanes* can also be linked to this type of literary circle without undue strain on the imagination.²⁵

Some casual minor allusions. Demonax is given a mild jest against the philosopher Apollonius, tutor-designate to the emperor,²⁶ and caustic comments on the poetaster Admetus and a medley of unnamed grammarians and philosophers.²⁷ The effeminate Bassus in *Adversus Indoctum* 23 may be a sophist with a pedigree.²⁸ Epigram 26 runs thus:

Εἰπέ μοι εἰρομένῳ, Κυλλήνιε, πῶς κατέβαινεν
    Λολλιανοῦ ψυχὴ δῶμα τὸ φερσεφόνης;
θαῦμα μέν, εἰ σιγῶσα· τυχὸν δέ τι καί σε διδάσκειν
    ἤθελε· φεῦ, κείνου καὶ νέκυν ἀντιάσαι.

It may or may not be Lucianic. Lollianus was a figure of importance and controversy. He came from Ephesus and was a pupil of Isaeus whose volubility (which irritated Juvenal and

---

24. Allinson, *Lucian*, pp. 18-20; he also has Apuleius participating in these soirées.

25. *Convivium* 40 has the Platonist Ion rebuked for a solecism by the rhetorician Dionysodorus; it would be congenial to equate Ion with Favorinus. Gellius, *NA* 9.4, waxes enthusiastic over his acquisition of a collection of second-hand books of *mirabilia* in Brundisium; their exotic contents recall the satire of Lucian's *Vera Historia*. Lexiphanes and his friends are antiquarian and hypochondriac.

26. *Demonax* 31. This was Apollonius of Chalcedon whom Antoninus summoned as tutor to Marcus Aurelius. He is remembered with affection in *Meditations*, 1.8, 1.17; the *HA*, *Antoninus* 10.4, has less favourable tales of his arrogance and greed. Dio, 71.35, has Nicomedia as his birthplace.

27. *Demonax* 44 (on the one-line epitaph composed for himself by the "vile poet Admetus"), 14 (a loquacious "Sidonian sophist"), 26 (a devotee of obsolete words).

28. *Adversus Indoctum* 23. On this and other Bassi see Bowersock, *Sophists*, p. 25.

delighted Pliny[29]) he inherited. He was appointed to an inaugural chair of rhetoric at Athens, where he shone in both sophistic and forensic eloquence. His performance as controller of the food supply and markets was less happily distinguished; in a riot, he was saved from a mob stoning by the epigrammatic intervention of Pancrates the Cynic.[30] This example of a professional sophist having to rely on borrowed eloquence for salvation is particularly entertaining, since one of Lollianus' most notable efforts was on the theme of Leptines and the shortage of food in Athens. The paradox was perfect grist to the mill of a Lucian.

Now Herodes Atticus: scholars are poles apart in their interpretations of his relationship with Lucian. For Allinson[31] he is "one of the few contemporaries actually singled out for praise by Lucian"; Bowersock and Schwartz see little love lost between the pair.[32] The evidence points to the latter view. Demonax makes two barbed references to Herodes' ostentatious grief over his wife Regilla and son Polydeuces.[33] True, Herodes is introduced in the first of these anecdotes as ὸ πάνυ. This is translated by Harmon as "the superlative," which is misleading; the phrase occurs elsewhere in Lucian,[34] and means "famous." The term would be complimentary or sarcastic according to the intonation of the speaker; it is relevant that Gellius can hardly ever refer to Herodes without a clutch of compliments and titles, a procedure which the sophist would do nothing to discourage.[35] The fractious relationship between Herodes and Fronto, notwithstanding their joint consulship of 143, suggests that Gellius was a host and

29. Pliny, *Epistulae* 2.3, has an enthusiastic account of Isaeus; he is proverbial for loquacity in Juvenal 3.74.

30. Philostratus, *VS*, p. 526. It is worth noting that Lollianus' diction is often criticised by Phrynichus (see, e.g., Rutherford, p. 65). He has a good press from Philostratus, but his habit of planting statues to himself in Athens may have provoked Lucian to ridicule.

31. Allinson, *Lucian*, p. 18.

32. Bowersock, *Sophists*, p. 115; Schwartz, pp. 32-3.

33. *Demonax* 24, 33.

34. *Vitarum Auctio* 22 (of Electra), *Apology* 5 (of Cleopatra).

35. Gellius, *NA* 1.2, 9.2, 18.10, 19.12. See Philostratus, *VS*, p. 564, for a good example of Herodes' vanity.

mediator of remarkable tact.[36] In *Peregrinus* 19, Herodes is described (though not named) as a man of outstanding attainments in literature and public office and as a benefactor to Greece for supplying water to Olympia and other amenities. But if Lucian had had any relish for Herodes, he would surely have reported the verbal deflation of Peregrinus as Philostratus does.

It is a minor tragedy that we cannot safely claim the *Nero* for Lucian, since the dialogue hinges on the projected cutting of the Isthmus canal. This was a scheme contemplated by Herodes but not executed.[37] Other points of similarity between Nero and Herodes commend themselves, such as the deaths of Poppaea and Regilla from blows in the stomach during their pregnancies and theatrical grief over deceased progeny. The *Nero* could have been classified as a recognisable satire on Herodes; and still can be, whoever the author was.[38]

The career of Herodes has often been documented.[39] Philostratus' account (very different from the occasional details of Gellius), supplemented by the admittedly partisan comments of Fronto, inspires distaste for the sophist. His vast inherited fortune, his treatment of Regilla and his freedmen and slaves, his perpetual quarrels (with Antoninus Pius, Marcus Aurelius, and the Quintilii), his swindling of the Athenians over the matter of the legacies (it is hard to believe Philostratus' account of the Athenian grief at his death), all command contempt. Herodes deserved a reserved place in the Lucianic Underworld with the tyrants and the millionaires.

Nothing much can be discovered about the shadowy philosophers Demonax and Nigrinus. The *Demonax* is introduced as a companion piece to a biography of a Boeotian called Sostratus who was of unusual height and strength and lived a Robin Hood

36. See Bowersock, *Sophists*, pp. 95-9, for Herodes and Fronto. Gellius keeps the two well apart in his *NA*.

37. Philostratus, *VS*, p. 551.

38. On the authorship see Bowersock, *Sophists*, p. 3; M. D. MacLeod in the Loeb *Lucian*, Vol. 8, 1967, pp. 505-7. Nero is the typical tyrant for Marcus Aurelius (*Meditations*, 3.16) and Epictetus (3.22). It was a stroke of luck for the biographer of Verus in the *HA* to discover that Verus and Nero shared their birthday.

39. Graindor; Day, pp. 241-51; Bowersock, *Sophists, passim*.

type of existence around Parnassus. He was known to the Greeks as Heracles, and could be identified with the Heracles-Agathion who lectured Herodes on the purity of rustic Greek. If so, the loss of Lucian's piece on him is regrettable, since it would have been a useful vehicle for passing adverse comment on Herodes. The *Demonax*, in fact, is essentially a convenient cover for ventilating typical Lucianic criticisms of Favorinus, Herodes, Peregrinus, and assorted grammarians and archaists. There is no need to doubt Demonax's existence, or that Lucian was personally familiar with him. Indeed, since his basic virtues are frankness of speech and an eclectic view of philosophic dogmas, he may be rated an important influence on Lucian's intellectual development. If so, Lucian felt his debt discharged by the biography; there is no other reference to him in the extant works.

Nigrinus the Platonist may be fact or fiction. There is the temptation to interpret his name as a semantic joke on Albinus, but the dangers inherent in seeing a question simply in terms of black and white are well known. Since Lucian allegedly visited Nigrinus in Rome in the course of his search for an oculist, it is worth noting that Galen has a reference to Albinus the Platonist in the context of a book on ocular diseases.[40] This clinches no arguments, but could be remarkable coincidence or no coincidence at all. It is adventurous to look for a connection with the hapless C. Avidius Nigrinus executed by Hadrian; were there one, it would be easy to understand why Lucian's Nigrinus became a philosopher recluse!

The addressees of certain Lucianic pamphlets are philosophers and problems. Cronius, the recipient of the *Peregrinus*, might be tentatively connected with the Cronius whose books were said by Porphyry to have been one of the influences on Origen.[41] Celsus is a more rewarding enigma. The scholiast on the *Alexander* equates

40. *De suis libris* 2.

41. Eusebius, *Historia Ecclesiastica* 6.19. But since Lucian, *De historia conscribenda* 21, claims that an Atticist historian would change Saturninus into Cronius, we may be on the wrong track altogether. Another character named, without affection, in the *Peregrinus* is the Cynic Theagenes, who has been equated with the Theagenes whose death is described by Galen; see Bernays, pp. 13-18.

the addressee of Lucian with the author of the Ἀληθὴς Λόγος:

οὗτός ἐστι Κέλσος ὁ τὴν καθ᾽ ἡμῶν μακρὰν φλυαρίαν ἐν
ὀκτὼ γράψας βιβλίοις, ᾧ πρὸς ἰσάριθμον ἀντεξαγόμενος
πρόθεσιν ὁ σπουδαιότατος ἀντεῖπεν Ὠριγένης, μεστοὺς
ἁπάσης σοφίας καὶ εὐσεβείας ἐξυφηνάμενος λόγους καὶ λῆρον
ἀποφήνας τὸ θαυμαστὸν αὐτοῦ σπούδασμα.

Origen himself believed Celsus to be an Epicurean who flourished
in the Antonine period,[42] and who also composed a treatise on
sorcery. Galen mentions an Epicurean Celsus in his bibliography.[43]
The scholiast's identification is commonly denied,[44] but Origen's
Celsus is the ideal addressee for Lucian. There could have been no
better audience for the account of Alexander's fake magic and the
unpredictable fellowship of Epicureans and Christians against the
prophet. It is likely that what little Lucian really knew about
Christianity came from Celsus; the latter must have derived unholy
pleasure from the *Peregrinus* also (of which he would have been
the ideal recipient).

Five familiar representatives of the second century remain as
candidates for inclusion in the gallery of Lucian's friends and
enemies. Aelius Aristides may have had reason to reckon Lucian
amongst the many ills afflicting him; Arrian and Fronto may be
extracted from the *De Historia conscribenda*; Galen will perhaps
emerge from the linguistic thickets of the *Lexiphanes*; the age-old
status of Pollux as butt of the *Rhetorum Praeceptor* could prove
to be suspect.

Boulanger[45] was right to say that "on ne peut découvrir chez
Lucien aucune allusion certaine aux discours ni à la personne
d'Aristide"; he was just as wrong in observing that

la manière oratoire d'Aristide . . . s'accordait assez bien avec

42. *Contra Celsum* 1.8.
43. *De suis libris* 16.
44. E.g., by M. Caster, *Etudes*; Chadwick, pp. xxxv-xl (he sees Origen's
Celsus as a middle Platonist rather than an Epicurean; but Origen, 1.8,
thought that Celsus dissembled over his Epicureanism so as not to deter some
of his readers); Frend. The identification was accepted by Keim.
45. A. Boulanger, "Lucien," pp. 144-51.

les principes littéraires de Lucien, et distinguait nettement l'orateur de Smyrne de ces charlatans de l'art oratoire dont l'ignorance et la mauvaise foi sont denoncées dans le Maître de Rhetorique.

The two could very well have met each other in Italy, Greece, or Egypt.[46] Lucian's *De Saltatione* may be a response to Aristides' diatribe against dancing. It has already been suggested that Lucian's piece may have been a compliment to Verus, thrown off at Antioch in the early 160s. Aristides was on good terms with Marcus Aurelius, and this emperor's dislike of dancing[47] may have been motive enough for the sophist's effusion. Although it proves nothing, later manuscript traditions tend to connect the two pieces.[48] It is also possible that the *Nigrinus* (and perhaps the *De Mercede Conductis*) can be taken as deliberately antithetical to Aristides' cliché-ridden *Roman Oration*.[49] Criticism of Aristides has also been detected by some in the *Rhetorum Praeceptor*,[50] and it would not be audacious to believe that Lucian found Aristides' mania for oracles and visions a source of amusement. If there was no formal connection between the two, we are certainly left with several very striking coincidences.

There is one unequivocal reference to Arrian by Lucian. In *Alexander* 2, he is described as the follower of Epictetus, a distinguished Roman, a life-long devotee of literature, and the author of a biography of the bandit Tillorobus.[51] The general phraseology is reminiscent of the cold allusion to Herodes in the

---

46. The main areas of Aristides' travels; see Philostratus, *VS*, p. 582.

47. *Meditations* 11.2; see Kokolakis, *Lucian, Pantomimus*, p. 9.

48. The Lucian defence is regarded as an answer to Aristides in Vaticanus 90, and is associated with the reply to Aristides by Libanius in this manuscript and the Vindobonensis; the Libanian defence occurs in both. See the Teubner *Libanius* of R. Foerster, 1908, pp. 406-419, and also J. Mesk, "Des Aelius Aristides verlorene Rede gegen die Tanzer," *Wiener Studien* 30, 1908, pp. 59-74.

49. See the controversial Peretti; Oliver; Baldwin, 1961, pp. 199-208.

50. L. Méridier, pp. 207-9.

51. Tillorobus appears in some manuscripts as Tilliborus. The theme would have been painfully topical; see MacMullen, pp. 255-68.

Peregrinus, and the restriction of reference to Arrian's productions to the otherwise unknown brigand's biography suggests that Lucian was not specially keen to praise him. Some have seen more covert allusions to Arrian in the philosophical governor of Syria in *Peregrinus* 14,[52] and the friendly governor of Cappadocia in *Alexander* 55.[53] By contrast, attempts to show a protracted polemic between the historian and the satirist are at least as convincing.[54]

One matter dividing them was Alexander the Great. The ridicule of Alexander's conquests and claims to divinity in the *Dialogues of the Dead* goes counter to Arrian's general principle of discounting evidence unfavourable to the Macedonian, and the Lucianic scorn of Aristobulus in *De Historia conscribenda* 12 as a venal flatterer equally sets the pair apart; so also does *De Domo* 1, where Lucian accepts the anecdote of Alexander's near-fatal dip in the Cydnus, a story given by Arrian as contrary to Aristobulus' version.[55]

The compilers of *Parthica* are said by Lucian to be self-conscious imitators of Herodotus, Thucydides, and Xenophon. An inevitable remark. However, although once praised in the pamphlet as a "just historian,"[56] Xenophon runs a poor third in the individual examples of bad imitation listed by Lucian (scribblers who write history without prefaces appeal to the authority of the *Anabasis*). Arrian prided himself on being the "New Xenophon"; a comparison of their respective works justifies this dubious accolade, and the title stuck to him in later Antiquity.[57] It is

52. G. A. Harrer, "Was Arrian Governor of Syria?," *CP* 77, 1916, pp. 338-39.

53. The equation is made in the *Index Rerum* of C. Jacobitz' Teubner *Lucian*, 1841.

54. H. Nissen, "Ueber die Abfassungszeit von Arrians Anabasis," *Rheinisches Museum* 43, 1888, pp. 236-257. He places the *De Historia conscribenda* in 165, the first two books of Arrian's *Anabasis* and the *De Domo* in 166, the *Dialogues of the Dead* in 167, and the remainder of the *Anabasis* in 168.

55. On Arrian see Bowie, pp. 24-8.

56. *De Historia conscribenda* 39; the only other significant reference to Xenophon is *Somnium* 17.

57. See Photius, *Bibliotheca* (*Cod.* 58), and Suidas. Arrian's picture of

questionable whether Lucian thought the title one to boast about. The issue recalls a previous point: just who was the Xenophon accompanying Lucian in the *Alexander?*

Imitation of Herodotus impinges upon the question. Lucian mocks two historians for attempting to reproduce Ionic Greek; one was the medical Callimorphus whose attempts at dialect fell away into linguistic anarchy, the other is unnamed.[58] Pseudo-Ionic had a revival in the second century,[59] and Lucian took advantage of the phenomenon for comic purposes.[60] Arrian's Ionic experiments in the *Indica* were, as Chantraine demonstrates,[61] something of a disaster.

Such are the grounds for supposing an unfavourable view of Arrian on Lucian's part. The position of Fronto is naturally equivocal. The reference to an anonymous would-be Thucydidean as ἀοίδιμος ἐπὶ λόγων δυνάμει has been taken to allude to Fronto,[62] and an unnamed Atticist had occasion to transmute the name Fronto into Phrontis in his ridiculed mania for transliterating Roman names into Greek.[63] I am not the first to see a possible connection between Fronto's *Principia Historiae* and Lucian's criticisms,[64] and one or two similarities of detail are adducible. For instance, Fronto begins by comparing Verus' exploits to those of Achilles, a conceit complained of by Lucian;[65] Frontonian flights

himself as the new Xenophon comes out in *Cynegeticus* 1.4; see Bowie, pp. 24-8, on Arrian's posturing in the fragmentary *Expeditio contra Alanos.*

58. *De Historia conscribenda* 16.18.

59. See Lindemann; F. G. Allinson, "Pseudo-Ionicism in the Second Century A.D.," *AJP* 7, 1886, pp. 203-17; Bompaire, pp. 630-32.

60. The *De Dea Syria* and the possibly authentic *De Astrologia* are written in Ionic. Herodotus speaks in his dialect in *De Domo* 20, as do the Pythagorean, Heracleitean, and Democritan philosophers in *Vitarum Auctio* 3, 13.

61. In the Preface to his edition of the *Indica*, 1952, pp. 11-12, 16-19, Chantraine concluded that "L'ionien de l'Indicé n'a aucune réalité linguistique," and that "L'ionien d'Arrien est purement artificiel."

62. By C. R. Haines, Loeb *Fronto*, Vol. II, 1929, p. 199.

63. *De Historia conscribenda* 21.

64. Brock, p. 65; J. Révay, "Un ouvrage perdu de Fronton," *Acta Academiae Hungaricae*, 1951, pp. 161-190 (I rely on the French résumé of the article which is in Russian).

65. *De Historia conscribenda* 14.

such as "catafractos similes esse beluis piscibus, eas eludere alto mari cernuantes . . . in magnis persultare campestribus" are akin to the poetic effusions which provoked Lucian's scorn; a hint that Fronto was aware of hostile critics is given in the mutilated section where Verus is elevated over Trajan by the words "haec a me detrectationis refutandae causa memorata sunt."[66] The position of Fronto in the circles of Gellius, Favorinus, and (their differences notwithstanding) Herodes Atticus marks him as a very likely target for Lucian. Personal animosities and sectarian disputes usually intertwine closely in Lucian, and there may as usual be more than meets the modern eye in the choice of historian-victims. Further speculation is idle, but hostility between Lucian and Fronto is a working possibility.

Pollux provides a change of pace. The scholiast knew of a tradition that made him the victim of the *Rhetorum Praeceptor*, though the identification was not an established fact. It has almost become one in modern scholarship, though there have been dissenters.[67] The dialogue is a satirical manual for aspirant orators. A young tyro seeks and hears advice from two professionals of very different ideals. The first is a representative of the old school, advocating hard work, constant practice, and unremitting study of classical Athenian models. The second speaker (the presumed Pollux) is a "typical" modern; he misuses and abuses the Attic models, preaches ignorance and insolence, and knows how to purchase fame and acquire undeserved wealth. He is furnished with some autobiographical details and character traits which are the basis for the equation with Pollux. His father was a slave in Egypt, his mother a seamstress in the slums. The orator was catamite to an elderly pederast (not a unique imputation in a Lucian pamphlet),[68] after which he graduated to the role of gigolo to a septuagenarian lady with four false teeth of gold. His more

66. *Principia Historiae* 17.

67. The classic study is Ranke. The identification is accepted by, e.g., Croiset, *Histoire* V, p. 645; Harmon, Loeb *Lucian*, Vol. 4, 1925, p. 133; Bompaire, p. 128. It is rejected by Boulanger, "Lucien," and by Méridier, who picks on Aelius Aristides.

68. The *Peregrinus*, *Pseudologistes*, and *Adversus Indoctum* are eloquent tributes to this Lucianic motif.

respectable fame was acquired in the courts.

The key passage for the identification is: οὐκέτι Ποθεινὸς ὀνομάζομαι, ἀλλ᾽ ἤδη τοῖς Διὸς καὶ Λήδας παισὶν ὁμώνυμος γεγένημαι.[69] Potheinus might suggest an Egyptian career, but the name is admirably suited to the orator's sexual versatility; its status as an occupational name for eunuchs has added comic possibilities. The sons of Zeus and Leda appear ideal for Pollux; in fact, there are serious objections. The translation "namesake" for ὁμώνυμος is legitimate, but not binding. It can imply similarity of name, bearing an exactly identical name, nickname, or fraudulent use of a name.[70] The plural παισὶν is strange if Pollux is meant; why not the singular? Boulanger[71] made the point crisply: "Rien n'est moins certain que cette identification. Le pluriel est fort surprenant si le mot de l'énigme est Pollux. Un nom comme Dioscoros ou Dioscorides conviendrait beaucoup mieux."

The Egyptian origins of the orator prove nothing. His father is associated with the towns of Xois and Thmuis, nome capitals in the Delta region; not an obvious reference to Naucratis. Nor was Pollux the only sophist to derive from Naucratis; Apollonius, Proclus, and Ptolemy (not forgetting Athenaeus) share the honour. Low birth has been perverted into an argument for Pollux, since Philostratus is reticent over the personal details of Pollux' origins. This is absurd; Philostratus was no great admirer of Pollux, still less was he shy of scabrous detail.[72] Unless Lucian was totally unscrupulous in his tirade, the slave-father cannot be reconciled with Pollux' father who, according to Philostratus, was an expert

69. *Rhetorum Praeceptor* 24.

70. See *Imagines* 10 (on Panthea), where the word must connote exact identity of name; Arrian, *Cynegeticus* 1.4, uses it to indicate his Xenophon nickname. For the cognate noun meaning "fraudulent use of a name" see *P. Oxy.* 1266.36 (an application for membership of a gymnasium, c. A.D. 98).

71. Boulanger, "Lucien"; unfortunately, where can we find a victim by either of these names? Harmon, Loeb *Lucian*, Vol. 4, 1925, p. 133, tried to explain the point away by saying that Lucian "may be a bit vague on purpose." This is not unreasonable in principle, although this section of the *Rhetorum Praeceptor* seems cruelly precise.

72. E.g., *VS*, p. 516, for anecdotes on the background of Scopelian. His attitude to Pollux is summed up in the final sentence: "He died at the age of 58, leaving a son who was legitimate but illiterate."

in sophistic who coached his son. Nor does the real Pollux have a great deal in common with Lucian's orator who is a compendium both of the traits of most sophists in Philostratus and of Lucian's other victims such as Lexiphanes.[73] The short specimens of his declamatory style given by Philostratus, and the prefaces to the volumes of the *Onomasticon*, exhibit no great abnormalities of style. The fact that the *Onomasticon* represents the sort of research ridiculed in the *De Saltatione* is inconclusive of anything.[74] Finally, Lucian's orator shone in the courts; Philostratus associates Pollux with sophistic declamation and philology. Regrettably perhaps, Pollux has to be dethroned from his position in Lucian's gallery of enemies. There is, of course, no implication that he be elevated to the status of friend.

The most intriguing possibility is a relationship between Lucian and Galen. There is no actual mention of the great doctor's name, but grounds exist for suggesting a compliment from Lucian to him in the *Lexiphanes*.[75] This dialogue is one of Lucian's most elaborate satires against one of the linguistic foibles of the second century, the mania for obscure and archaic Attic diction. The two protagonists are the foppish and foolish Atticist, Lexiphanes (the "Word-flaunter," as A. M. Harmon dubbed him in his Loeb translation), and his old friendly neighbourhood enemy, Lycinus, who as usual appears as the triumphant mouthpiece for his creator's views. After some preliminary backchat from Lycinus, Lexiphanes reads an increasingly unbearable extract from his new masterpiece, a *Symposium* à la Plato. His soporific droning is eventually interrupted by the desperate Lycinus, who follows up an initial criticism of Lexiphanes' style by calling in the doctor,

73. *Rhetorum Praeceptor* 16 and *Lexiphanes* 21 share one or two cant words from the Atticists. The orator advises the use of obscure words, which is obviously congenial to Lexiphanes, but only a smattering of Attic terms is recommended. Another piece of advice is to brazen out any solecism or barbarism which may be detected; this exactly fits the sophist Philagrus of Cilicia (Philostratus, *VS*, p. 578) who, when challenged to cite an authority for an allegedly outlandish word, made the excellent retort: "In Philagrus."

74. *De Saltatione* 33 ridicules antiquarian research and pedantic detail.

75. This dialogue is ascribed to the period 165-75 by, e.g., Croiset, *Lucien*; Schwartz, p. 149, with more confidence than evidence posits it in 176, and Bouquiaux-Simon, p. 26, refers the piece to after 175.

Sopolis, who administers a purge which forces the Word-flaunter to vomit up his cherished Attic vocabulary. Sopolis then hands back the patient to Lycinus for further formal criticism and a final prescription for literary success.

This piece of Sopolis-opera has left some mark on English letters. The purging scene is used by Ben Jonson in *The Poetaster* and by Thomas Dekker in his *Satiromastix*. It is also agreeable to find the pert Fanny Burney dubbing Dr. Johnson "Lexiphanes"; fair comment on the sage who dazed his audiences with such sesquipedalian efforts as "anfractuosity," "papilionaceous," "labefactation," and the like. Walpole's comment on "the teeth-breaking diction of Johnson" also serves as a pretty description of the original Lexiphanes.

Patient before doctor. The actual identity of Lexiphanes is a relevant problem that cannot be shirked. Any approach should be antithetical to that of Bompaire who, playing down the contemporary relevance of Lucian's satire as usual, claims:[76]

"Quant au *Lexiphane*, il est, autant qu'un coup porté à l'hyperatticisme, une caricature du Banquet de Platon; Lucien s'est laissé entraîner, en la composant, au-delà de ce que la seule observation des travers atticistes lui permettait.

This judgement arises out of his almost totally false statistics for Lexiphanes' hyperattic diction.[77] The mock *Symposium* is not a haphazard jumble of words from Attic Comedy, as Bompaire maintains; it is carefully put together by Lucian to include a good number of usages which are discussed, disputed, and animadverted against by Phrynichus of Bithynia, Moeris, and, in particular, Cynulcus, the enemy of Ulpian and Pompeianus of Philadelphia in

---

76. Bompaire, p. 483.

77. Bompaire, pp. 634-6. For instance, Lexiphanes employs the word ἱπνολέβης, described by Bompaire as "mot qui utilise ἱπνός particulièrement familier à Aristophane." That may be true, but is quite irrelevant; the point is that in Athenaeus (3.98c), the word is a cant term with the Ulpianean Sophists for the Roman μιλιάριον or water-heater. Bompaire further says of fancy neologisms that they are "peu nombreux parceque répondant mal au but de l'ouvrage." In cold fact, there are thirty-four in just under six Teubner pages.

Athenaeus' *Deipnosophistae* (3.97c). At least nine words used by Lexiphanes, both in his conversation and his literary confections, are usages criticised in the Athenaeus section.[78] Seiler and Harmon[79] are very likely right in regarding Lexiphanes as representing Pompeianus or the Ulpian school in general. Alternatively, Lexiphanes may be designed to make the audience think of Phrynichus; the latter's pretentious and ignorant pedantry spring to mind when Lexiphanes claims in his *Symposium* that he and his prolix friends are "the quintessence of Atticism."[80] And we shall see that Phrynichus and medical men did not love each other.

Extracting real people from literary disguises is a dangerous business. However, Sopolis may be a compliment to Galen. The doctor's career has been fully worked out elsewhere,[81] and only a few pertinent reminders are needed for this discussion. He was born in 129 and came to Rome in the early 160s after extensive travels; his desire to leave Pergamum may have been quickened by the epiphany there of poor Aristides. From one plague to another. He left Rome in or after 166, but the great epidemic caught up with him at Aquileia in the winter of 168-9. After his return to Rome, he served the emperors and their courts until his death in 199.

The name Sopolis commands attention. It is registered as a new entry in the *Supplement* to Liddell-Scott-Jones as an epithet of Apollo or the name of a deity; the allotrope Sosipolis occurs as an epithet bestowed upon a human benefactor. Although it has been asserted that the plague was not an important part of Galen's practice, nor one of his prime interests,[82] the notion that Sopolis' name might be a compliment to Galen for his work during the plague can be toyed with.

Galen is a natural ally in Lucian's "fight" against the Atticist

78. The vocabulary of Lexiphanes is more fully discussed later.

79. See Harmon, Loeb *Lucian*, Vol. 5, 1936, p. 291, for discussion of the point.

80. *Lexiphanes* 14; such smugness is obviously universal, from Gellius' circle to the French Academy.

81. See Walzer; Sarton; Bowersock, *Sophists*, pp. 59-75.

82. By J. F. Gilliam, "The Plague under Marcus Aurelius," *AJP* 82, 1961, pp. 225 ff.

plague. He wrote a large number of works on language. The diction of Old Comedy emerges as a major interest, and there is, significantly, a polemical title against the spotters of solecisms.[83] Galen also ridicules critics who specialise in discovering alleged solecisms in the speech of others; he suggests that moral laxness is more to be condemned than verbal.[84] He penned a treatise on clarity and ignorance, and is on record as regarding σαφήνεια as the prime literary virtue; Lycinus orders Lexiphanes μάλιστα δὲ Χάρισι καὶ Σαφηνείᾳ θῦε. Galen also has biting comments on that type of ῥῆσις where the thought is adapted to the words, not the words to the thought. The point has obvious general application to the practitioners of the second sophistic who had moved a long way from *rem tene, verba sequentur*, but the identical criticism is made against Lexiphanes at some length.[85] Of special relevance is Galen's objection to the purist demands for Atticist style from philosophers, mathematicians, and medical men. Phrynichus is often scornful of the diction of medicals in the *Praeparatio Sophistica*; De Borries was probably right to suggest that the purists had a *nota cum medicis de sermone contentio*.[86] The fur flew for a good while, as is shown by such items as the *Antiatticistes* pamphlet and the anonymous comment preserved in Walz' *Rhetores Graeci*[87] that Phrynichus' teaching was "nonsense" and the critic himself "worthless." Another observation by Galen may not indeed have been entirely to Lucian's taste, but is germane: Atticist expertise for its own sake has no intrinsic virtue.[88] Galen's cavilling against the social éclat of Atticism is equally striking.[89] Finally, as Walzer has pointed out, Galen's

83. *De suis libris* 17: πρὸς τοὺς ἐπιτιμῶντας τοῖς σολοικίζουσι τῇ φωνῇ.
84. *De ordine suorum librorum* 5: ἀπαξιῶ μηδενὶ μέμφεσθαι τῶν σολοικιζόντων τῇ φωνῇ μηδ᾽ ἐπιτιμᾶν· ἄμεινον γάρ ἐστι τῇ φωνῇ μᾶλλον ἢ τῷ βίῳ συλοικίζειν τε καὶ βαρβαρίζειν.
85. *Lexiphanes* 24.
86. In the Preface to his Teubner edition, p. xxvi.
87. Vol. 5, p. 610.
88. *De ordine suorum librorum* 5: ἡ τῶν Ἀττικῶν ὀνομάτων γνῶσις οὐδὲν αὐτὴ καθ᾽ ἑαυτὴν ἄξιον ἔχουσα μεγάλης σπουδῆς.
89. *Ibidem*: οὐ γὰρ δὴ τοῦτ᾽ ἀξιοῦμεν ἡμεῖς, ὅπερ ἔνιοι τῶν νῦν κελεύουσιν, ἅπαντας ἀττικίζειν τῇ φωνῇ, κἂν ἰατροὶ τυγχάνωσιν ὄντες ἢ φιλόσοφοι καὶ γεωμετρικοὶ καὶ μουσικοὶ καὶ νομικοὶ κἂν μηδὲν τούτων ἀλλ᾽

antipathy to the dogmatic attitudes of contemporary sects can be related to Lucian's position in the *Hermotimus.*[90]

There is no warrant for running amok and claiming that the character of Sopolis was a compliment to the influential Galen, designed to win a patron; or that it was a way of thanking the great man for procuring Lucian's Egyptian appointment. Still less should we build a vision of Galen tending the gouty satirist.[91] Such things are tempting, and not impossible, but it may be safest to propose that the bond between Lucian and Galen was intellectual rather than personal. Whatever the connection, Galen can be listed in the catalogue of Lucianic friends (or allies).

ἀπλῶς ἤτοι πλουτοῦντές τινες ἢ μόνον εὔποροι· For a collection of these and other relevant passages in Galen see Herbst. An anonymous grammarian routed by Fronto in Gellius, *NA* 19.10, is a good example of linguistic snobbery: "Nam nescio quid hoc praenimis plebeium est et in opificum sermonibus quam in hominum doctorum notius."

90. Walzer, p. 7.

91. Lucian is generally respectful towards medicine and its practicioners. See, e.g., J. D. Rollestone, "Lucian and Medicine," *Janus* 20, 1915, pp. 86-108; H. Crosby, "Lucian and the Art of Medicine," *TAPA* 54, 1923, pp. 15-16. But it would be a pity to forget the comment in Athenaeus, 15.666a: εἰ μὴ ἰατροὶ ἦσαν, οὐδὲν ἂν τῶν γραμματικῶν μωρότερον.

Three
The War of the Words

Lucian is nowhere less original than in his dialogues and diatribes on the literary practices and linguistic foibles of the second century.[1] Philological in-fighting was widespread; it is one of the commonest motifs in Aulus Gellius, the anecdotes of Philostratus, and the lexicographers such as Phrynichus and the *Antiatticistes*; Fronto is evidence for its popularity as the sport of kings.

Lucian's most striking feature in this context is a negative one: his virtual neglect of Latin topics. The age tended to prize bilingual expertise as a cardinal virtue.[2] Gellius scorned a Greekless questioner as an *opicus*,[3] a relatively mild example of the snobbery and cruel humour attending the principle. Favorinus bequeathed to Herodes a wretched Indian slave called Autolecythus, whose clumsy efforts at Greek were a source of amusement to Herodes and Favorinus.[4] Herodes' crack at Peregrinus' poor Greek, men-

1. For a general sketch of the conventions see B. A. Van Groningen, "General Literary Tendencies in the Second Century A.D.," *Mnemosyne* 18, 1965, pp. 41-56.

2. Aulus Gellius is star witness to this; see, e.g., *NA* 1.2 (on Herodes), 8.2 (on Favorinus). Lucian (*De Mercede Conductis* 24-5) speaks of the bad Latin of the hireling scholar (bad accent or indifferent command of the language?) who is needed to give his master the requisite gloss of the two cultures. The phenomenon is obviously not to be restricted to the second century; we need only recall the libraries of Trimalchio.

3. *NA* 11.16; the monoglot applied to Gellius for assistance over a book of Plutarch.

4. Philostratus, *VS*, p. 490. The anecdote is reminiscent of Petronius,

tioned previously, was inspired more by malice than linguistic concern, but underlines the point. The matter was one affecting emperors as well as slaves; here there is some refreshing balance. Dio saw bilingual competence as one of Hadrian's chief virtues, contrasting with Trajan who was deficient in "culture in the strict sense."[5] Philostratus' anecdote about Trajan not understanding Dio Chrysostom is not usually believed, and has perhaps been misunderstood; it is not always easy to shut a philosopher up, and Trajan's "I do not understand what you are saying, but I love you as myself" may prove tact rather than ignorance of Greek on his side.[6] Favorinus is credited with the ability to charm even Greekless audiences, though it may sometimes have been to the listener's advantage not to understand the mellifluous eunuch.[7] Most intriguing is the need felt by the young Marcus Aurelius to defend his interest in Greek against some strictures by Fronto.[8] It hardly needs stating that Marcus was not deflected from his Greek; he did, however, commit the singular offence of using a word objected to by the pedantic Phrynichus.[9]

Why Lucian elected to play down Latin issues is not altogether clear. *Pro Lapsu Salutandi* 13 is clear evidence that he had a working knowledge of the language, something we could reasonably have assumed anyway without joining the old hunt for allusions to Juvenal in the *Nigrinus* and *De Mercede Conductis*. His debatable anti-Roman sentiments may be part of the answer, though I do not care too much for that particular solution; allusions to Latin matters are not logically precluded in an anti-Roman writer.[10] One illuminating fact is that Lucian's

Satyricon 68, where a slave's attempts to recite Virgil evoke sour amusement from Encolpius.

5. Dio Cassius, 69.3 (Hadrian), 68.4 (Trajan: the criticism is restricted to his oratory).

6. *VS*, p. 488; See Bowersock, *Sophists*, pp. 47-8.

7. *VS*, p. 491. These episodes took place in Rome.

8. Haines 1.18: "Graece nescio quid ais te compegisse, quod ut aeque pauca a te scripta placeat tibi. Tune es qui me nuper concastigaras, quorsum Graece scriberem? Mihi vero nunc potissimum Graece scribendum est."

9. Haines 2.291: the word was γλωσσόκομον (see Rutherford, p. 181).

10. See Bowie, pp. 15-18, for the Greek attitude to Roman history. It is not surprising that Lucian reinforces his claim to a knowledge of Latin by

comments on style arose as much out of personal conflicts as from
ideological conviction. In this, he was typical of the second
sophistic. As we have seen, and shall see again, the *Lexiphanes* was
aimed at the Ulpian sophists who take a notable drubbing from
the Cynic Cynulcus in the *Deipnosophistae*. The *Rhetorum
Praeceptor, Pseudologistes,* and *Soloecistes* are all vicious and
personal diatribes. He was capable of lighter, impersonal comments such as those in the *Demonax* and *Convivium*; the clever
fooling of the *Iudicium Vocalium* and the jokes on traditional
Homeric scholarship in the *Vera Historia* can also be adduced.
However, the *Pro Lapsu Salutandi* and the *Pseudologistes* show
that Lucian himself was vulnerable to the same sort of attack. His
satire, at least in part, is as much defensive as offensive.

The literary interests and involvements of emperors and courts
furnished another excellent reason for satire on such themes. It
was a sure way to attract an influential eye, though the danger of
saying the wrong thing was not always far away if one had not
done one's homework ahead of time. Trajan is hardly relevant to
Lucian, but can be inserted here with great pleasure and some
pertinence. The Philostratean anecdote concerning him and Dio,
and his falling between the two stools of Suetonius and the
Historia Augusta, suggests that he was odd man out in the
tradition of imperial men of letters. Yet he was surely the only
emperor ever to receive a secret message in Latin written on a
giant mushroom.[11]

Hadrian's artistic versatility is notorious, and there is no need
to dwell on his philhellenic enthusiasms here. The popular image
of a more respectable Nero is short of the truth. Some of his
opinions (if he was serious) were refreshingly unorthodox; the
reaction of Homeric scholars to the news that the epic genius was
inferior to Antimachus of Colophon must have been wonderful to
behold. His preference for Cato over Cicero and Ennius over Virgil
(there is a slight smack of Caligula here) seems in tune with the

introducing an anecdote on Augustus (*Pro Lapsu Salutandi* 18). In *Dialogues
of the Dead* (12.7), Lucian perhaps confuses Scipio Africanus with
Aemilianus. Roman names are included in the *Octogenarians*, though the
listing is mechanical.

11. Dio Cassius, 68.8. There is scope here for Mr. John Allegro.

tastes of Fronto. However, it is notable that Fronto had no high opinion of Hadrian's judgement. He tells Verus that "veteris eloquentiae colorem adumbratum ostendit oratio."[12] Hadrian had a pronounced capacity for feuding with men of letters; he would be quite at home in a learned journal. There were clashes with Favorinus and Dionysius of Miletus, and moments of awkwardness with Herodes. The reader of Gellius' *Noctes Atticae* will not be sorry to find Favorinus worsted by the emperor over a point of pedantry.[13] Other literary worthies drawn into the issues were Avidius Heliodorus, the poet Florus, Epictetus, and a host of anonymous victims of the emperor's sharp pen and astringent tongue. The gallery is too much for the biographer of the *Historia Augusta* who gets himself into marvellous muddles over details.[14] The general picture of Hadrian can look suspiciously like a compound of Julio-Claudian traits from the pages of Suetonius; his habit of asking awkward questions of rhetoricians and philosophers is obviously comparable to the similar pastimes of Tiberius. Accept the account, and one can begin to understand the unsympathetic portraits of Hadrian; no professor relishes tricky questions. Hadrian was a sophist with a real empire, a character with whom Lucian would have found a good deal in common. The emperor's deathbed words provide a final and pertinent little puzzle. Did he die composing verses or cursing doctors?[15]

We have already seen Antoninus Pius in action against greedy philosophers and the haughty sophist Apollonius. The picture lends credibility to the statement of the *Historia Augusta* that he reduced the salary of Mesomedes the lyric poet.[16] In Philostratus,

12. Haines 2.138.

13. *HA, Hadrian* 15.12. Dio Cassius, 69.3, and Philostratus, *VS*, p. 489, assert a fractious relationship between Hadrian and Favorinus; see Bowersock, *Sophists*, pp. 51-2.

14. E.g., Heliodorus is assailed by Hadrian in a slanderous pamphlet (*Hadrian* 15.5) and treated with great cordiality later on (*Hadrian* 16.10).

15. The deathbed verses to his *animula* (reported only by *HA, Hadrian* 25.9-10) are rejected by T. D. Barnes in *CQ*, 18, 1968, pp. 384-6. Barnes prefers Dio Cassius, 69.22 (epitome by Xiphilinus), where Hadrian dies with the shout that many doctors have killed a king. For arguments against Barnes see my rejoinder in *CQ*, 20, 1970, pp. 372-374.

16. *HA, Antoninus* 7.8; other unspecified persons were also deprived of their alleged sinecures.

Antoninus normally appears in disputes with sophists; he is found in conflict with Polemo, Herodes (this episode is not believed by Philostratus), and Alexander "Clay-Plato."[17] Lucian's conventional tribute to Pius has already been noted; nothing disrespectful to the emperor is expected or found in Fronto. The lack of sources obstructs any clear view of Pius, but the glimpses afforded by Philostratus lead to the unexpected conclusion that, at least in encounters with sophists, he was not all that different from Hadrian. The last word goes to Marcus Aurelius who, apart from confirming Pius' sharp treatment of dubious philosophers, observes that no one would call him a sophist or a pedant.[18]

Marcus Aurelius appears in many of Philostratus' anecdotes involving luminaries such as Polemo, Herodes, and Aristides.[19] With Fronto he is polite, considerate, and tactful. Interesting hints are dropped in the *Meditations* on his real feelings towards some of those to whom he was deferential in public. Of his literary mentors, he singles out Alexander of Cotiaeum for teaching him not to censure solecisms or other literary vices in others; mention of Fronto follows, but there is no tribute to the latter's literary precepts; Herodes is notably excluded.[20] It would be tempting to believe that Marcus' opinions were influenced in his later years by Galen (and by reading Lucian?); this can only be conjecture, but Marcus' selection of teachers for mention in his *Meditations* (philosophers dominate at the expense of orators and grammarians), his gratitude to Rusticus for warning him away from rhetoric, poetry, and precious style, and his above mentioned comment on Pius, combine to suggest a growing exasperation with sophistic practices or practicioners.

17. *VS*, p. 534 (Polemo), p. 554 (Herodes), p. 570 (Alexander). The first two incidents occurred before Antoninus became emperor.

18. *Meditations*, 1.16: καὶ τὸ μηδὲ ἄν τινα εἰπεῖν μήτε ὅτι σοφιστὴς μήτε ὅτι οὐερνάκλος μήτε ὅτι σχολαστικός.

19. *VS*, p. 540 (Polemo), p. 559 (Herodes), p. 582 and 583 (Aristides).

20. See Farquharson's note on *Meditations*, 1.16. Alexander of Cotiaeum is mentioned in *Meditations*, 1.10, and is listed as one of Marcus' teachers in *HA, Marcus Antoninus* 2.3; for his relationship with Aristides see Behr, pp. 10-11. The relationship between Fronto and Herodes has been discussed earlier. Fronto's absence from Philostratus and the lack of interest in Herodes on the part of the *HA* are perhaps notable omissions.

The truth about Verus (to borrow a pun from Fronto and the *Historia Augusta*) is beyond recall. He is credited with poetry and oratory, affection for his teachers (dutifully reciprocated), and a natural lack of literary abilities.[21] His one appearance in Philostratus is tantalising: Marcus suspects him of plotting with, among others, Herodes.[22] The possibility of a connection between Verus and Lucian was earlier explored. Commodus is not often suspected of academic interests, thanks to the *Historia Augusta*, but a slight corrective is supplied by the other sources. His liquidation of the Quintilii was inspired by distrust of their learning which he felt might drive them to radical feeling; however, he was charmed by the more flexible sophist, Hadrian of Tyre, and the latter's wordy pupil, Pollux.[23]

Finally, a twist is provided by Avidius Cassius. His father was the successful man of letters, Avidius Heliodorus from Syria. The son rose and fell in abortive revolt against Marcus Aurelius in 175. One of his complaints against Marcus was that the emperor spent too much time on philosophy whilst the state suffered; familiar words to modern ears.[24] We recall the celebrated note rushed to Avidius by Herodes. The latter had nothing to gain if Avidius prospered, but if it was true that he had clashed with Antoninus Pius in days gone by and had been suspected of connivance with Verus, he perhaps needed to demonstrate his loyalty in good haste. In view of his record, and the fate of the Quintilii (unless he

21. *HA, Verus* 2.4-9. The claim that Verus was "melior quidem orator fuisse dicitur quam poeta, immo, ut verius dicam, peior poeta quam rhetor," perhaps imitates Quintilian's verdict on Lucan.

22. *VS*, p. 560. The *HA* naturally lists Herodes (with Fronto) as one of Verus' teachers. This tradition was apparently not followed by Dio Cassius, 71.1-2; Dio couples Herodes and Fronto as Marcus' teachers without comment on their personalities (71.35).

23. See earlier for the Quintilii; on Commodus and the sophists Hadrian and Pollux see Philostratus, *VS*, p. 590 and p. 593.

24. *HA, Avidius* 3.5 (where Marcus is dubbed as *dialogistam*), and 14.5 (an alleged letter from Avidius to his son-in-law after the revolt; the document is probably spurious, but the sentiment is notable). Dio Cassius, 71.35, asserts that Marcus' philosophic zeal prompted large numbers of charlatans to pursue philosophy in the hope of imperial patronage. Lucian's *Piscator* echoes this situation.

THE WAR OF THE WORDS 47

could have turned his feud with them to good account), one wonders what would have happened between Herodes and Commodus. One wonders all the more what were the thoughts of Lucian on the revolt of a fellow Syrian (not that the ethnic label should be pressed too far in actual relevance) who was weary of philosophers.

It is clear that Lucian's satire on linguistic topics is inside, not outside, the conventions of the period. It is necessary to distinguish between Atticism, antiquarianism, and archaism, The terms are not synonymous in practice, and their equation has led to confusion. Harmon, for instance, in his introductory comments to the *Lexiphanes*, saw the cult of rare words as a feature of Latin rather than Greek, and named Fronto as the leading devotee.[25] In fact, Fronto is cautious on the issue. Although he favours *colorem sincerum vetustatis*, he sums up his basic principle thus: "Ego immo volgaribus et obsoletis (*sc.* utor). Quid igitur est? Nisi istud saltem scirem, deterioribus uterer."[26] The qualification is important; Lexiphanes would have died rather than use a common word. Equally striking is the evidence of Gellius. His interest in antiquarian matters and arcane information co-existed with a scorn of excessive archaism in contemporary speech and writing. The following sermon from Favorinus makes the point abundantly:

> Favorinus philosophus adulescenti veterum verborum cupidissimo et plerasque voces nimis priscas et ignotas in cotidianis communibusque sermonibus expromenti: "Curius," inquit, "et Fabricius et Coruncanius, antiquissimi viri, et his antiquiores Horatii illi trigemini, plane ac dilucide cum suis fabulati sunt neque Auruncorum aut Sicanorum aut Pelasgorum, qui primi coluisse Italiam dicuntur, sed aetatis suae verbis locuti sunt; tu autem, proinde quasi cum matre Euandri nunc loquare, sermone abhinc multis annis iam desito uteris, quod scire atque intellegere neminem vis quae dicas. Nonne, homo inepte, ut quod vis abunde consequaris, taces? Sed antiquita-

25. Loeb *Lucian*, Vol. 5, 1936, p. 291.
26. Haines 2.80. For a good example of Fronto in linguistic debate see Gellius, *NA* 19.8.

tem tibi placere ais, quod honesta et bona et sobria et modesta sit. Vive ergo moribus praeteritis, loquere verbis praesentibus atque id, quod a C. Caesare, excellentis ingenii ac prudentiae viro, in primo De Analogia libro scriptum est, habe semper in memoria atque in pectore, ut tamquam scopulum, sic fugias inauditum atque insolens verbum."[27]

A friend of Gellius is stigmatised as "homo in doctrinis, quasi in praetigiis, mirificus communiumque vocum respuens."[28] Favorinus' sermon is restated by Gellius thus:

> Verbis uti aut nimis obsoletis exculcatisque aut insolentibus novitatisque durae et inlepidae, par esse delictum videtur. Sed molestius equidem culpatiusque esse arbitror verba nova, incognita, inauditaque dicere quam involgata et sordentia. Nova autem videri dico etiam ea quae sunt inusitata et desita, etsi sunt vetusta.[29]

Gellius traces the vice to ὀψιμαθία. The Noctes Atticae reflect several of Lucian's favourite topics: ignorant critics of language and false philosophers stand out as specially relevant.[30] As with Lucian, the victims are not usually named. This correlation of themes must not lose sight of the fact that Lucian was antipathetic to the luminaries of Gellius' circle. He was outside the coteries, inside the conventions.

Emperors, Atticists, sophists, antiquarians united in ridiculing the archaists. Time has been harder on the victims. By a common irony, their reputation survived through the barbs of the critics; the same is true of Lucian's hapless compilers of Parthica. A word of defence is needed to redress the balance. The revival of archaic words was not in itself a vice. In our own day, lexicographers such

27. NA 1.10.
28. NA 7.15.
29. NA 11.7.
30. See e.g., NA 1.10, 4.1, 6.17, 7.16, 8.10, 9.2, 11.7, 14.5, 15.9, 18.4, 19.1, 19.10. Critics praised by name include Sulpicius Apollinaris, Antonius Julianus, Aelius Melissus (praised as a grammarian, but disparaged as a literary critic, in NA 18.6), Julius Paulus the poet, Annianus the poet, and Taurus the philosopher. A notable victim of Favorinus is the grammarian Domitius, nicknamed "Insanus" (NA, 18.7).

as Ivor Brown in his Word Books have enriched the English
language by recalling words from the First Elizabethan age to the
second. An exotic epithet from Shakespeare or a Johnsonian
polysyllable can be a good deal more attractive than a piece of
cant sociological jargon from the sixties. To kill off old words is
no better a principle than to massacre old ideas. Moreover, Lucian
himself with his "moderate Atticism"[31] was just as much an
archaist in principle and in practice. His approach to style was
equally mandarin and equally likely, on his own first premises, to
contribute to the sterility of the Greek language.

Nor should we be too quick to sneer at antiquarianism. To see
Aulus Gellius as the symptom of an intellectual disease hardly
befits the classical scholar. The *Noctes Atticae* resemble nothing so
much as the pages of a learned journal. Scholars today are sensitive
to taunts that their discipline is "out-of-date" or "irrelevant." We
do not grant the charge against ourselves, and have no right to
throw these accusations against Gellius and company. Critics may
be parasitic on the arts, and we may be tempted to agree with
Housman on literary criticism (especially if we have been the
victims of a hostile review). The fact remains that philology and
lexicography have a universal importance. Gellius and his kind
were a symptom of health, not sickness.

Dogma and pedantry were more deserving of ridicule. The
least attractive phenomena of the second century were critics such
as Phrynichus of Bithynia. For Lucian's sake, I hope that
Phrynichus and his ilk were the real targets of the *Pseudologistes*
and the *Soloecistes*,[32] and of Galen's strictures against the
seekers-out of "solecisms." Philostratus did well to deny Phrynichus (and Moeris, if he was of the period) a place in his gallery.
Laying down the law as to what constituted "good Attic" and
what was not was a greater threat to the development of Greek
than the revival of old words as a stylistic device. The troubles of
modern Greece over Katharevousa and Demotic (what side would
Lucian have been on?) bear sad witness to this. Phrynichus struck
the postures of a blinkered Englishman raving against the alleged

31. See Chabert and Deferrari for statistics.
32. This point is argued later, with statistics.

corruptions of American English (the type can still be found, in spite of the fact that British English is peripheral in terms of the number of people speaking English of one sort or another). It is a keen pleasure to discover that he (like Lucian) does not live up to his principles in his own writing.[33]

Lucian devotes two dialogues (accepting, for the moment, that the *Soloecistes* is genuine), one defensive diatribe (the *Pseudologistes*), and one piece of impersonal fooling (the *Iudicium Vocalium*) to the subject. Although archaism is one detail, the *Rhetorum Praeceptor* is basically a portmanteau skit on sophistic themes and practices and is excluded from the present discussion.

Lexiphanes is in linguistic trouble with his very first words, describing his latest production as τητινόν. The epithet is sanctioned by Phrynichus as sound Attic, and occurs in Pollux, although the only other source cited in the Lexicon is the grammarian Herodian.[34] The analagous expression ἡ τῆτες ἡμέρα is criticised in Athenaeus by Cynulcus as an affected archaism of Pompeianus of Philadelphia, one of the group of sophists around Ulpian. This is the first of several verbal links between Lexiphanes, Phrynichus and the Atticist purists, and the Ulpian circle. Lexiphanes is soon in trouble again with Lycinus, when he claims εὔλεξις as a virtue of his *Symposium*. This is a fetish prescribed by the *Rhetorum Praeceptor* in his recommendations for archaic diction: ἐνίοτε δὲ καὶ αὐτὸς ποίει καινὰ καὶ ἀλλόκοτα ὀνόματα καὶ νομοθέτει τὸν μὲν ἑρμηνεῦσαι δεινὸν "εὔλεξιν" καλεῖν, τὸν συνετὸν "σοφόνουν," τὸν ὀρχηστὴν δὲ "χειρίσοφον."[35]

The following words used by Lexiphanes are instructive:

(a) καύματα: Used in the sense of "frosts." This is another expression of Pompeianus ridiculed by Cynulcus.[36]

---

33. See Rutherford, p. 493, for comment on an example of Phrynichus' style.

34. Phrynichus, *Praeparatio Sophistica*, p. 114 (in the Teubner edition of De Borries). Suidas defined the epithet as equivalent to χθεσινός.

35. *Rhetorum Praeceptor* 17.

36. *Deipnosophistae* 3.98b. C. B. Gulick's Loeb version translates as "burnt-offerings," which ignores the context of winter clearly brought out in the passage. Schweighaeuser correctly explained the meaning: "Ferventem

(b) ἀπολούμενος: This Attic contraction of ἀπολουόμενος to produce confusion with the future of ἀπόλλυμαι is derided in both Ulpian and Pompeianus.

(c) συντριβέντες: Used in the sense of "rubbed down after a bath." Another favourite term of Pompaeianus.

(d) ξύστρᾳ: Used here in the sense of "comb." The word is confirmed by Pollux, but rejected by Phrynichus.[37]

(e) ἱπνολέβης: A cant term with the Ulpians, discussed in the previous chapter.

(f) ἄδικος ἡμέρα: The phrase is used to mean "a day when the courts are closed." Cynulcus criticises its use by Pompeianus.

(g) ὀπτός: This is used by Lexiphanes to mean "visible," but could cause confusion with ὀπτός in the sense of "roasted." Another Pompeianus speciality.[38]

(h) ἄχρηστα and ἀφόρητα: The first is used to mean "unused," the second to mean "unworn." Both are expressions favoured by Pompeianus.

Lexiphanes describes the menu of his *Symposium* in terms as rich as the food. Bompaire offers "statistics" for several of these to prove his contention that Lucian "a consulté un lexique des comiques ou tout au moins d'Aristophane, moyen mécanique au service de la parodie."[39] I append the terms in question, Bompaire's "statistics," and the truth.

(a) ὀκλαδίας and ἀσκάντης: "Substantifs employés seulement par Aristophane." The first occurs in Pausanias and an inscription, the second in the Palatine Anthology.[40]

(b) ἠτριαία: "Exclusivement Aristophanesque." The word is used by Athenaeus (1.4c).

---

aestum dicens cum frigus urens vellet dicere." The Lexiphanes usage is unequivocal.

37. Rutherford, p. 358.

38. Athenaeus elsewhere (8.338c) gives another example of the possible pun from the grammarian Chamaeleon.

39. Bompaire, p. 635.

40. The general references in this section follow the latest edition of Liddell-Scott-Jones.

(c) τάγηνον: "Uniquement comique." Lucian uses it himself (*Convivium* 38); the orthography of the word is discussed by Ulpian and Aemilianus (Athenaeus, 6.228) and also by Pollux (10.98).

(d) μυττωτός: "Aristophanesque et post-classique." It can be found in Hipponax and Hippocrates.

(e) ἀβυρτάκη: "Exclusivement comique." It is used by Nymphodorus and Polyaenus.

(f) σαργάνη: "Comique et post-classique." In fact, the word occurs in sources as diverse as Aeschylus, the New Testament, and papyri of the third and fourth centuries.

Lexiphanes' diction was carefully selected by Lucian to fit the perspectives of contemporary coteries and dogmatisms. Both the pedantry and ignorance of Phrynichus and the cant vocabulary of the Ulpian clique are constantly recalled. It cannot be claimed as a certainty that Lexiphanes represents Pompeianus or Ulpian in particular, but the similarities between the Lucian and Athenaeus portraits are suggestive. It is self-evident that Ulpian and Pompeianus are luminaries of a coterie. Lexiphanes is the centre of admiration from his circle of fools (*Lexiphanes* 17). Ulpian is portrayed as a rigid and intolerant purist, quick to take offence and quicker to give it. Epithets bestowed upon him include φιλάρχαιος and συραττικός. His nickname Κειτούκειτος derives from his habit of questioning the authority of words in both public discussion and at private parties (Gellius gives a similar picture of Fronto; in *NA* 19.10, for example, whilst suffering from gout and discussing the cost of building baths with a group of architects, he drops everything to challenge the word *praeterpropter*). Examples of his interrogations include two words discussed by Phrynichus.[41] He is pardonably ready to hit back at the Cynics' own diction and is querulous about his fellow grammarians. In turn, both he and Pompeianus are ridiculed as "word-hunters" and "word-coiners." Ulpian is notably censured for lacking χάρις in his

41. Can μέθυσος be applied to a man? See Rutherford, p. 240 (also Pollux, 6.25). Can σύαγρος be applied to a boar? Phrynichus (Rutherford, p. 476) denied the usage; contrast the discussion in *Deipnosophistae* 9.401a, where Sophocles and Antiphanes are cited.

diction, a virtue Lexiphanes is urgently advised to cultivate along with clarity. The picture conforms on every point to Lexiphanes who is the object of ridicule from critics and very ready to take the offensive in philological debates.

Pompeianus is unknown outside Athenaeus and it is hard to decide whether Ulpian is the celebrated jurist or the latter's father; the father is more appropriate chronologically to the *Lexiphanes*.[42] The parallels between Ulpian and Fronto cannot be dismissed, but it was earlier established that Fronto was not an extremist in archaism. The *Lexiphanes* was topical satire; Bompaire's interpretations should be returned to the vacuum of his *Mimesis*.

In the *Soloecistes*, Lucian shows up the pretensions of an unnamed expert in the detection of solecisms by stunning him with a flood of subtle and not so subtle violations of "strict Attic usage." The attack is reinforced by a long list of alleged solecisms exposed and ridiculed by Lucian's former acquaintance or teacher in Egypt, Socrates of Mopsus. The dialogue closes with the chastened critic undertaking to concede his reputation and accept instruction from Lucian.

The construction of the dialogue is similar to the *Lexiphanes*. Socrates of Mopsus is assigned the role played by Sopolis in the latter, and the critic is reduced to the status of patient. This general affinity extends to one or two linguistic details; Lucian and Socrates each condemn a usage ridiculed in Lexiphanes; in both cases there is agreement with Phrynichus.[43]

---

42. The identification with the jurist was proposed by Schweighaeuser (followed by Kaibel and Gulick; Bowersock, *Sophists*, p. 14, n. 4, is undecided) on the basis of Ulpian's last words in *Deipnosophistae* 15.686c, which allegedly anticipate his death in 228. But Athenaeus' Ulpian ἀπέθανεν εὐτυχῶς, which hardly suits the account of the jurist's violent death in Dio Cassius, 80.2. Ulpian in Athenaeus is known as the "Tyrian"; this accords with the jurist's origins, but proves nothing. The presence of the jurist as one of the *docti homines* favoured by Severus Alexander (*HA, Alexander* 34.6) is predictable. On the possibility of Ulpian the father see W. Dittenberger, "Athenaeus und sein Werk," *Apophoreton* 1903, pp. 1 ff. It is worth noting that there was a sophist Ulpian at Antioch who was one of Prohaeresius' teachers, and Suidas has an Ulpian of Emesa who wrote on rhetoric.

43. The usages are ἵπτασθαι (Rutherford, p. 373) and καθέζεσθαι (Rutherford, p. 336).

The authenticity of the dialogue has been denied on three grounds. The name "Lucianus" is very rare, if not unique, as a substitute for Lycinus in the dialogues. Emotional reaction against the alleged dullness of the piece has led to its rejection. Most compelling is the fact that many of the usages criticised by Lucian and Socrates are found elsewhere in Lucian.[44]

The first two objections are easily tackled. Manuscript evidence on the *dramatis personae* is fragile; Nilén's apparatus shows that the names are absent from many of the manuscripts.[45] In fact, the alternative title is *Pseudosophistes*; whether this is genuine and/or significant is impossible to decide. Dullness, if granted, is not a cogent reason for rejecting the piece as spurious. Lucian was all too capable of waxing tedious on linguistic points, especially if his argument was coloured by personal malice or if he was on the defensive.

The third argument is a serious one. There are ten clear cases of Lucian condemning Lucianic usages; eight further Lucianic usages are criticised by Socrates; one final example seems to prescribe an orthography condemned elsewhere by Lucian. It is equally alarming to find Lucian and Socrates in agreement with the prescriptions of Phrynichus of Bithynia in almost a dozen cases.[46]

Macleod proposes four possible interpretations which might reconcile genuine Lucianic authorship with this situation. First, Lucian identified himself with the views expressed in the piece. He had improved and modified his knowledge and opinions concerning Attic style, and was aware that he was condemning

44. The point is fully documented by M. D. Macleod in the Loeb *Lucian*, Vol. 8, pp. 4-45, and in his article in *CQ* 6, 1956, pp. 102-111.

45. See also A. Bellinger, "Lucian's Dramatic Technique," *Yale Class Stud* 1, 1928, pp. 3-40.

46. They concur on ἄρτι with the future (Rutherford, p. 70), the intransitive use of διέφθορα (Rutherford, p. 246, where Phrynichus condemns the usage as typical of ignorant medical writers), πήνικα for πότε (Rutherford, p. 122), κορυφαιότατος (Rutherford, p. 144). ἐξεπιπολῆς (Rutherford, p. 205), συντάττομαι with the dative (Rutherford, p. 75), συγκρίνομαι with the dative (Rutherford, p. 344), false application of καρῆναι (Rutherford, p. 368), ἔκτοτε (Rutherford, pp. 116-17), βράδιον (Rutherford, p. 149), the intransitive use of ἀνέῳγε (Rutherford, p. 246).

himself. The association with Socrates may suggest a relatively late date for the dialogue. This theory is vulnerable on several grounds. If the dialogue indicates a conversion to pedantry, it is odd that Lucian would have let it circulate along with the *Lexiphanes*, *Rhetorum Praeceptor*, and *Pseudologistes*. The expression ᾧ συνεγενόμην ἐν Αἰγύπτῳ, relating to Socrates, may mean "of whom I have seen a great deal in Egypt," but the verb can also imply consultation with a person on one specific occasion.[47] Nor is it impossible that Lucian had been in Egypt before his civil service appointment. Moreover, if he is serious in objecting to several attested Attic usages, the dialogue makes no sense. Macleod anticipated this point and suggests that Lucian is only criticising usages "opposed to current educated practice." But this involves another paradox, since the whole ideal of Phrynichus and company was to re-establish what they thought was real Attic, and to censure any deviation from this norm.

The second possibility is to assume that Lucian was pandering to an audience of ill-informed experts and simply suppressed his own views and knowledge that many of his criticisms were invalid. Lucian was certainly capable of trimming some of his sails to the winds of patronage, but not usually in the area of linguistic satire. Hypocrisy here is hard to reconcile with the sound and fury of the *Lexiphanes*, *Pseudologistes*, and *Adversus Indoctum*.

A third interpretation, which Macleod prefers, is that Lucian is attacking a particular enemy so ferociously that he lost all sense of proportion and was totally hypocritical in censuring his own usages for the sake of his diatribe. The weakness of the dialogue is explained by the poor quality of his victim and by the presumption that the dialogue was written in his old age. Again, Lucian was perfectly capable of ill-proportioned malice, but I doubt that he could have been so slovenly or willing in leaving himself open to counterattack. Macleod adduces the *Pseudologistes* as a prime example of Lucian's hypocrisy in refusing to admit a linguistic error on his own part; however, as will be seen, Lucian had not made a mistake at all. The correlation of old age

---

47. E.g., Aristophanes, *Aves* 113. However, Lucian says ἐπὶ μήκιστον συνεγενόμην of Demonax (*Demonax* 1).

with intellectual decline is a dangerous principle (we need only invoke Sophocles) which cannot be used to prove anything.

The fourth theory, which goes back through Reitz to the scholiast,[48] is the most attractive. Lucian is exposing the ignorance of contemporary purists and pedants by a *reductio ad absurdum* of their claims to be able to detect solecisms and establish an incontrovertible canon of Attic style. This view is most compatible with the construction of the dialogue where Lucian produces solecisms which the self-styled expert cannot recognise. It is in harmony with such passages as *Lexiphanes* 25 and *Pseudologistes* 29, where the same situation occurs or is alluded to; hoisting linguistic engineers with their own petard is a favourite Lucianic device. After his initial discomfiture, the expert grumbles: σὺ δ' οὐδὲν εἶπας ὧν ἄνθρωποι σολοικίζοντες λέγουσιν. A little later, Lucian slips in two daggers at once when he tells his victim: σὺ δὲ ὑπὸ τῆς ἄγαν παιδείας διέφθορας (this intransitive use of the verb is condemned here and also by Phrynichus). An enthusiastic reader of the dialogue would have been Galen who would have relished the mock condemnation of ἄν with the future, a construction verified in Lucian by Macleod and claimed by Hall as a peculiarity of Galen's own style.[49] The *Soloecistes* may well have been an appropriate companion to Galen's pamphlet against the seekers of solecisms.

The *Pseudologistes* may be relevant to any attempt to identify the butt of the *Soloecistes*. I published an article on this pamphlet some years ago,[50] and the following remarks summarise my conclusions. The victim was a sophist and fellow Syrian who ridiculed Lucian's use of the word ἀποφράς. Modern critics have

48. See Macleod, p. 108; Reitz was not disposed to believe his own suggestion. The scholiast explained the dialogue's purpose thus: σοφιστήν τινα εἰσάγει ἀπαίδευτον μεγάλα φρονοῦντα καὶ ἐπαγγελλόμενον ἅπαντα εἰδέναι τὰ σόλοικα. ὁ οὖν Λουκιανὸς βουλόμενος αὐτὸν ἐξελέγξαι μηδὲν εἰδότα ἑαυτὸν εἰσήγαγε σολοικίζοντα καὶ διὰ τοῦτο ψευδοσοφιστὴν αὐτὸν ὠνόμασεν.

49. Macleod, p. 107; Hall, p. 152. See also Tackaberry, pp. 83-5; Shewring, "Platonic influence in Lucian's *Clausulae*," *Berliner Philologische Wochenschrift* 28, 1934, pp. 814-16; B. J. Sims, "Final Clauses in Lucian," *CQ* 2, 1952, pp. 63-73; C. W. E. Miller, 'Τὸ δέ in Lucian," *TAPA* 42, 1911, pp. 131-45.

50. "The *Pseudologistes* of Lucian," *Class Rev* 12, 1962, pp. 2-5.

THE WAR OF THE WORDS   57

sided with the sophist. Wrongly: Lucian's defence is entirely justified.[51] The sophist's career is typical of a Lucian victim. He had a colourful sex life, made a disastrous public appearance as a public performer, and was both an ignorant pedant and a devotee of far-fetched diction. In the latter context, he shares a word with Lexiphanes,[52] and was guilty of a solecism condemned in the *Soloecistes*.[53]

Macleod suggests various possible links between the victims of the *Lexiphanes*, *Soloecistes*, *Pseudologistes*, and *Adversus Indoctum*. The critic of the *Soloecistes* may be the *Pseudologistes* or he may be Lexiphanes. Identification with the target of the *Adversus Indoctum* is also possible. Syrian birth is attributed by Lucian to both the *Pseudologistes* and the victim of the *Adversus Indoctum*; Lucian's relish for attacks on fellow Syrians may or may not be significant. Relevant to Macleod's scheme is Ulpian (father or son) who came from Tyre. These connections are not implausible, although there is no indication that Lexiphanes is a Syrian, and the butt of the *Adversus Indoctum* is unlikely to be the *Pseudologistes* since the former was duped by fake editions of classical authors whilst the latter made money out of such forgeries. It is probably better to distinguish between the Phrynichus school of pedantry and purism which is the most logical target of the *Soloecistes*, and the Ulpian sophists with their far-fetched diction which suits the *Lexiphanes*. Lucian's refusal to name names and the overlap of linguistic details (in addition to the affinities between the Ulpians and Fronto) precludes any final solution.

The *Iudicium Vocalium* is a clever piece of impersonal foolery

51. Harmon, Loeb *Lucian*, Vol. 5, p. 372, n. 1, and Bompaire, p. 472, n. 5, confuse Lucian's explanation of his alleged error (*Pseudologistes* 1) with his actual expression (*Pseudologistes* 8). Lucian did not actually say ὅμοιος ἀποφράδι, but ὃς φανεὶς ἔοικε τὴν ἡδίστην ἡμέραν ἀποφράδα ἡμῖν ποιήσειν. His expression was justified by Eupolis' ἄνθρωπος ἀποφράς. Harmon's notion that Lucian may not have known the Eupolis passage is unlikely; in *Pseudologistes* 15, Lucian says he could have cited the authorities but will not further expose his enemy's ignorance.

52. ῥησιμετρεῖν, which occurs in *Lexiphanes* 9.

53. πέταμαι for πέτομαι, although the reading in *Soloecistes* 7 is uncertain.

on the question of orthography. Sigma impeaches Tau before the court of the Seven Vowels for stealing the words spelled with double Tau. This piece of double-talk has been rejected as spurious,[54] but on no good grounds. The parody is quite in the Lucianic manner with its travestied decree, the allotropes of legal phraseology, the high-flown rhetoric, jests and invective, and the deposition of false evidence.[55] The suggestion that Lucian drew on the Γραμματικὴ Τραγῳδία of Callias is attractive, but the piece is more than a simple confection of haphazard accusations.[56] The suit ranges beyond the dispute between Sigma and Tau (incidentally, Lucian's own practice, as shown by Deferrari,[57] is largely on the side of Tau), and several of the disputed orthographies appear in the prescriptions of Phrynichus and other critics.[58] The question of dialect has been seen to be a theme of Lucian's satire before, and it was a common topic with critics and grammarians.[59] Nothing is further from the truth than Bompaire's conclusion:

> Dans le *Jugement des voyelles* il s'oppose curieusement à la tradition attique, en défendant le *sigma* contre le *tau* qui l'a pourtant supplanté en de nombreux cas dès l'époque classique; mais là encore il s'amuse (en sens inverse de tout à l'heure), il ne donne pas une leçon suivie, il fait vivre une marionnette, le sigma. Lucien ne s'intéresse à la polémique autour de l'Atticisme grammatical que pour en tirer des effets comiques.[60]

54. By Harmon, Loeb *Lucian*, Vol. 1, Introduction, p. ix; *ibid.*, p. 395. He offers no reason for his view.

55. For the mock legal phraseology see F. W. Householder, "Mock Decrees in Lucian," *TAPA* 71, 1940, pp. 199-216.

56. M. Brozec, "De Calliae Tragoedia grammatica," *Bulletin of the Polish Academy at Cracovia*, 1938, pp. 111-14; see also P. D. Arnott, "The Alphabetic Tragedy of Callias," *CP* 55, 1960, pp. 178-80. Callias' piece is known from Athenaeus, 7.276a, and 10.453c.

57. Deferrari, pp. 1-4.

58. Phrynichus discusses βασίλισσα (Rutherford, p. 306) and κολοκύνθη (Rutherford, p. 498); μυρρίνη is claimed as the true Attic form by Moeris.

59. Notably in Sextus Empiricus who specifies the study of dialects as one of the grammarian's duties (*Adversus Grammaticos*, 1.78), and agreed with Lucian and Galen on pedantry and the search for solecisms.

60. Bompaire, p. 142.

Lucian's satire on linguistic topics is based on personal animus and convention. The same acrimony is manifest on the Latin side in Gellius, and on the Greek in Phrynichus and the *Antiatticistes*.[61] Its presence amongst the sophists commemorated by Philostratus has been remarked earlier. The animus of Lucian and other polemicists sometimes blurs the real distinction between Atticist, antiquarian, and archaist. The omission of Lucian and Phrynichus by Philostratus is significant as well as ironic, as is the absence of Galen, the ambivalent verdict on Pollux, and the slighting of Hermogenes. The second century was an age of healthy literary controversy marked by a constant clash of principles and personalities. No part of Lucian's output was more contemporary in application; or more conventional in inspiration.

61. See K. Latte, "Zur Zeitbestimmung des *Antiattikista*," *Hermes* 50, 1915, pp. 373-94; also F. Jacoby, "Γενέσια: a forgotten Festival of the Dead," *CQ* 38, 1944, pp. 65-75. The *Antiatticistes* may have been a contemporary response to Phrynichus. The author defends 21 usages condemned in the *Praeparatio Sophistica*, and 148 Lucianic usages. The wide selection of sources justifies Jacoby's definition of the author as a Classicist rather than an Atticist. He ranges from Homer and Hesiod to Middle and New Comedy; the inclusion of Xenophon and Menander are clearly aimed at the narrow Atticism of Phrynichus.

Four
The Loud Speakers

Oratory in the second century was not restricted to school-room and theatrical display. The real world co-existed with the sophistic dream world of fourth-century Athens, and provided the orators with opportunities for advancement and distinction. Lucian had experience of forensic eloquence, a branch of the art looked down upon by many sophists and of small consequence in Philostratus. His success or failure cannot be measured, but the experience left a recognizable mark. Lucian had a weakness for presenting himself as an intellectual martyr, and used a courtroom setting with himself as defendant in the *Bis Accusatus* and the *Piscator*. Both dialogues are more informative on his career than the thinly autobiographical *Somnium*. His expertise was turned to literary effect in the *Iudicium Vocalium*, and to practical ends in his Egyptian position; *Apology* 12 is clear evidence that his chief duties were concerned with litigation.

Such a career was in no way unique. Nicetes of Smyrna and his pupil Scopelian of Clazomenae are attested by Philostratus; it is notable that both were Asianists and both were subject to abuse.[1] Another legal man was the versatile Lollianus of Ephesus; again an

---

1. Philostratus, *VS*, p. 511 (Nicetes), p. 519 (Scopelian). Nicetes combined sophistic and forensic expertise, but was allegedly reluctant to address the assembly of Smyrna. He clashed most notably with Roman financial officials, which would not harm his local standing. Philostratus found it necessary to begin his account of Scopelian with a defence of the sophist against his detractors. Scopelian and Nicetes were further remarkable in that they included tragic and epic poetry in their activities.

Asianist. It may have been in Smyrna that Lucian saw the equivocal attractions of the courts as a possible short cut to reputation and patronage.

Municipal politics were far from dead. Though insular, civic affairs were well worth involvement. Local distinction might lead to participation in an embassy to the emperor. Such a role satisfied the claims of fantasy and ambition. An orator could see himself as Demosthenes going to confront Philip; the situation lent substance to the most fashionable themes of the age, and perhaps helped to account for their popularity. There is no evidence that Lucian appeared on any such mission, even less that he would have refused the opportunity. As he himself felt bound to point out, the *De Mercede Conductis* was not to be taken as a reflection on imperial service. Nothing was more typical of Lucian's career than his own translation.

The consulships of Fronto and Herodes in 143 were only the supreme manifestation of intellectuals in the corridors of power. Unquietly flow the dons in the pages of Philostratus and the other sources. Nicetes was sent by Nerva to Gaul to resolve an old issue with the consular Rufus who had been unpopular in Smyrna over his financial exactions; Scopelian appeared on many missions, including the affair of Domitian's edict on vines; Smyrna, which had a pronounced preference for appointing sophists to embassies, replaced the aged Scopelian with Polemo; Marcus of Byzantium enchanted the difficult emperor Hadrian on a mission from his native city; Alexander "Clay-Plato" was sharp with Antoninus Pius when appearing for Seleucia, but is later found acting in a diplomatic capacity for Marcus Aurelius; Aristides reduced Marcus to tears over the fate of Smyrna, though he had on a previous occasion taken the precaution of packing his audience with applauding pupils before appearing before this emperor.[2] The frequent appearance of sophists as royal tutors and in the imperial secretariat is unsurprising.[3] Lucian's expression of hope for a

2. *VS*, p. 512 (the mission of Nicetes), p. 520 (Domitian and the vines), p. 521 (Polemo replaces Scopelian), p. 530 (Marcus of Byzantium and Hadrian), p. 570 (Alexander and Antoninus), p. 582 (Aristides on the fate of Smyrna), p. 583 (Aristides' hired applause).

3. See Bowersock, *Sophists*, pp. 43-58, for the phenomenon. Bowie, p.

provincial governorship was not excessively optimistic in principle, especially in Egypt which had seen the sophists Heliodorus and Valerius Eudaemon as prefects.⁴ As we have seen, this eminence of sophists was a phenomenon which might have been rudely shattered, had the revolt of Avidius Cassius been successful. Whether Avidius owed his distaste for intellectuals to incompatibility with his father, or to hopes of making appeal to some anti-intellectual element in the military, is a matter for speculation.

Oratory was equally important to those outside the "Establishment." Cynicism has been described as the "Philosophy of the Proletariat." This is an over-simplification. Demonax is praised by Lucian for his ability to disperse riotous mobs,⁵ and it was the cynic Pancrates who saved Lollianus from the stones of the hungry Athenians. By contrast, Peregrinus is blamed for fomenting an anti-Roman movement in Greece.⁶ Lucian on Peregrinus is not easily trusted, but his claim in the *Fugitivi* that cynics were stirring up the poor against their masters mirrors a state of affairs found earlier in Dio Chrysostom. Dio, rather like Lucian, combined sympathy for the poor with distaste for extremist action.⁷ Other peacemakers of note were Apollonius of Tyana who quelled a riot at Aspendos, and Polemo who calmed the factions of Smyrna.⁸

6, stresses the connections between oratory and the real world.

4. The evidence is assembled by Bowersock, *Sophists*, pp. 50-51, and O. W. Reinmuth, "A Working List of the Prefects of Egypt 30 B.C. to 299 A.D.," *Bulletin of the American Society of Papyrologists* 4, 1967, pp. 95-6. Both men were advanced from the office of *ab epistulis*. Hadrian's relationship with Heliodorus has already been discussed; Dio Cassius, 71.22, states that the sophist was appointed to Egypt as reward for his oratorical talents. Valerius Eudaemon is another example of confused or shifting relationship with the emperor. *HA, Hadrian* 15.3, claims that Eudaemon had helped Hadrian to the principate, but was later reduced to poverty by him. Some of Hadrian's apparent oddities are discussed by W. Den Boer, "Religion and Literature in Hadrian's Policy," *Mnemosyne* 8, 1955, pp. 123-44.

5. *Demonax* 9. On the subject in general see Dudley.

6. *Peregrinus* 19. The incident may be equated with the revolt in Achaia under Antoninus reported by *HA, Antoninus* 5.5.

7. Dio, *Orations* 7.103, 32.9, 43.7, 50.3.

8. *Life of Apollonius* 7.15; *VS*, p. 531.

Lucian has little to say on the phenomenon of intellectuals in high places. His attitude to individuals such as Herodes was based on personality issues rather than principles. His material success was modest by the side of Philostratus' luminaries. Fame in Gaul, a legal career in the East, and a functionary's role in Egypt were not likely to dazzle many people. His ambitions were conventional for any age. It is not surprising that he is more concerned to attack the militant cynics. The gap between sophist and cynic was comparable to the current one between professor and student radical. Lucian was looking to the former for his audience; the abundance of personal issues and literary sects ensured that satirical opportunities were not precluded. There was no serious incompatibility between this conformist programme, his use of Menippus as protagonist in the comic dialogues, and genuine (but theoretical) concern for social questions. We have seen before, and will see again, that sympathy for the poor was an acceptable convention; provided, of course, that sympathy was not translated into violent action.

The theory and practice of sophistic oratory naturally afforded Lucian his best satiric opportunities, and also scope for exhibiting his serious views on the current literary fashions. The question of oratorical models is a logical place to begin. Precedents tended to be as important to the orator as to the dogmatic Atticist lexicographers. Not for nothing did Lucian affect displeasure in the *Zeuxis* and *Prometheus es in verbis* at the praises bestowed on his "originality."[9] The point is underlined in the *Bis Accusatus* and the *Piscator*; Lucian is concerned to show that he has adapted and improved the old, rather than invented something new and disparate like a centaur.[10] Indeed, perhaps the greatest miracle ascribed to Apollonius of Tyana is his advice to Scopelian to develop an original style.[11]

When precedents become models, canons are not far away.

9. Both seem to be preambles to epideictic displays. The *Prometheus* is concerned with Lucian's comic dialogues.

10. The point is laboured with the same centaur conceit in *Bis Accusatus* 33. The *Bacchus* is anothe; introductory piece used for the same general theme.

11. Apollonius, *Epistle* 19 (in the Philostratus biography).

However, this is the moment to dismantle that old field-piece, the Canon of Ten Attic Orators. The work was begun by A. E. Douglas[12] who demonstrated that Cicero and Quintilian did not defer to the supposed orthodoxies of Alexandria, Pergamum, or Caecilius of Cale Acte. Douglas erred only in his conclusion that the canon "did not reach a final and fossilised form until the second century of our Era." The evidence points to a continued state of warfare over the canon throughout the second century. It was a contest in which Lucian fired not a few shots.

Antiphon and Andocides are ignored by Lucian.[13] Lysias is mentioned twice; both passages refer to the Socratic criticisms of his speech.[14] The theme is a commonplace with Gellius and Fronto.[15] Isaeus is included in a λαμπρὸς κατάλογος of orators in the relatively undistinguished company of Alcidamas, Isocrates, and Eubulides.[16] Isocrates rates four further mentions, only one of which is in a work of undisputed Lucianic authorship.[17] The cardinal allusion is *Rhetorum Praeceptor* 17 where the villain of the piece dismisses him as λῆρος; the context may imply Lucian's own good opinion. Lycurgus appears once, branded a coward.[18] Hyperides is rarely mentioned, and then roughly.[19] Six references to Aeschines are flavoured by Demosthenic allusions to his low birth and cowardice, slightly balanced by the statement that Philip was impressed by his erudition, and his dismissal by the *Rhetorum Praeceptor*.[20] Dinarchus is ignored. Demosthenes is a special case

12. Douglas, pp. 30-40.

13. An almost complete table of references is assembled by Householder.

14. *De Domo* 4, *Amores* 24.

15. Fronto mentions the topic in a Greek letter to Marcus Aurelius (Haines 1.20) and in his *Laudes Fumi et Pulveris* (Haines 1.42); Gellius, *NA* 1.9, 2.5 (quoting Favorinus on the differences between Plato and Lysias).

16. *Demosthenis Encomium* 12; see later for the authenticity of this dialogue.

17. *Demosthenis Encomium* 10 (reference to his Helen), *Octogenarians* 23, *Parasitus* 42 (his cowardice), *Rhetorum Praeceptor* 17.

18. *Parasitus* 42.

19. *Demosthenis Encomium* 31 (treachery to Demosthenes), *Parasitus* 42 (cowardice), *Parasitus* 56 (his *apologia*). There may be a pun on his name in *Demonax* 48.

20. *Somnium* 12 (son of a flute girl, but respected by Philip for his

and will be considered later. Other orators mentioned include Gorgias, Hippias, Prodicus, Polus, and Pericles.[21]

These individual references are notable for their restricted interest. Of the Ten, setting aside Demosthenes, only Isaeus, Isocrates, and Aeschines can be said to be commended for their actual oratory, and then only casually or by implication. Outside the Ten, Pericles is most carefully discussed. There is a reasonable inference that Lucian was far more interested in the later Attic orators than the early ones. If a canon was recognised, its members were not equally rated.

There are two possible references to a canon of Ten. One is a simple mention of τῇ ᾿Αττικῇ δεκάδι as a yardstick for culture and erudition.[22] The second is in the disputed *Amores* where two standards of oratorical persuasion are Pericles and τῶν δέκα ῥητόρων τὰς Μακεδόσιν ἀνθωπλισμένας γλώσσας.[23] Obviously this cannot be the orthodox canon, since none of the earlier orators could be said to be armed against Macedon. There seems to be a connection with a passage in Plutarch,[24] where the number of orators whose surrender was demanded by Alexander was variously given as eight or ten. Literary canons may well have been confused with or born out of historical episodes.

Lucian's contemporaries were equally unready to abide by any one orthodoxy. Apart from the Lysias commonplace, Fronto mentions only Demosthenes.[25] Gellius thought highly of Aeschines, pays a tepid compliment to Isocrates, and has the obligatory praise of Demosthenes together with the usual anecdotes.[26]

---

learning), *Parasitus* 42 (a traitor), *Parasitus* 56 (his *apologia*), *Apology* 7, *Adversus Indoctum* 27, *Pseudologistes* 27 (references to the impeachment of Timarchus, though the last of these is uncertain), *Rhetorum Praeceptor* 10 (son of a schoolmaster).

21. The self-starvation of Gorgias is registered in *Octogenarians* 23. Hippias, Prodicus, and Polus are given a collective mention in *Herodotus* 3. Pericles' oratory is praised in *Demosthenis Encomium* 20 and *Amores* 29; Thucydides' necrology is cited in *De Saltatione* 36. One other reference occurs in *Demosthenis Encomium* 37.

22. *Scythian* 10.

23. *Amores* 29.

24. *Demosthenes* 23; see Douglas, pp. 37-8.

25. He is the model orator (Haines 1.128).

26. *NA* 18.3 (Aeschines as "acerrimus prudentissimusque oratorum"),

Apuleius has a single compliment for Demosthenes.[27] The meagre evidence of the Latinists is strengthened by Greek sophistic practice and technical criticism. Hermogenes cites all the traditional ten orators, but they receive diverse estimates. Antiphon makes one appearance in favourable circumstances, whereas Andocides is only half-heartedly defended against certain critics.[28] Lysias receives detailed attention over and above the inevitable *Phaedrus* context; his style is commended for qualities such as δεινότης;[29] in these discussions, he comes out well from comparisons with Isaeus (mentioned only in this context) and Hyperides. The latter was no favourite of Hermogenes, although special mention is made of the poetic qualities of his *Deliacus*.[30] Isocrates receives a detailed critique, and is often cited;[31] the same attention is bestowed upon Aeschines.[32] Dinarchus comes off badly; the description of him as a κρίθινος Demosthenes is approved.[33] Demosthenes is naturally the perfect model; he is styled as τῷ κορυφαίῳ and his name is applied adjectivally to various technical elements of the rhetorical art.[34] Gorgias, Critias, and Pericles also receive some attention.[35] Hermogenes has one reference to a canon of Ten, but later Critias is joined with the Ten as an equal.[36] It is clear that Hermogenes did not regard the supposedly traditional canon as binding upon his taste, and his occasional polemical tone suggests that a final orthodoxy was far from established.[37]

The other evidence supports this claim. Two canons of ancient

10.18 (Isocrates), 10.19 (praise and citation of Demosthenes). For the usual anecdotes see 1.5, 1.8, 3.13, 8.9, 11.9.

27. *Apologia* 15, where the orator is "primarium dicendi artificem."

28. For convenience I cite these Hermogenes passages by reference to the pagination of H. Rabe's Teubner edition, 1913. The Antiphon reference is on p. 400.

29. Pp. 297, 324, 347, 376, 377, 387, 395, 396, 407.

30. Pp. 243, 347, 395, 396, 401.

31. P. 397 for a detailed study; see Rabe's index for the many allusions.

32. P. 397 for a special critique.

33. P. 399.

34. P. 396 for the accolade; Rabe's index runs to almost six columns on Demosthenes.

35. Pp. 249, 377 (Gorgias); pp. 33, 401, 403 (Critias); p. 373 (Pericles).

36. P. 403.

37. E.g., p. 429, for apparent hits at contemporary notions.

orators, and one contemporary gallery, are recognised by the
Aristides *Prolegomena.*[38] It is natural to suppose that the older
Attic orators were Phrynichus' models.[39] The citations of the
Antiatticistes are predictably quirky.[40] The comparative tables of
Householder indicate that Lucian's interests were commonplace,
though he was more inclined than some to neglect Lysias.[41] An
anecdote of Philostratus has Herodes hailed as "one of the Ten";
the sophist rejoined that he was at least better than Andocides.[42]
Herodes is also regarded by Philostratus as greatly influenced in his
sonority by Critias. The biographer of the sophists himself
certainly recognised no fixed canon, in spite of the above allusion
to one.[43]

38. Lenz, p. 111: Τρεῖς φοραὶ ῥητόρων γεγόνασιν, ὧν ἡ μὲν πρώτη
ἀγράφως ἔλεγεν, ἧς ἐστι θεμιστοκλῆς καὶ Περικλῆς καὶ οἱ κατ᾽ ἐκείνους
ῥήτορες, ἡ δὲ δευτέρα ἐγγράφως, ἧς ἐστι Δημοσθένης καὶ Αἰσχίνης καὶ
Ἰσοκράτης καὶ σὺν αὐτοῖς ἡ πραττομένη τῶν ῥητόρων δεκάς. καὶ αὗται οὖν αἱ
δύο φοραὶ ἐν ᾿Αθήναις γεγόνασιν, ἡ δὲ Τύχη καὶ τῆι ᾿Ασίαι τούτων δωρεῖται
φοράν, τρίτην οὖσαν ἐπιστήμην, ἧς ἐστι Πολέμων, ῾Ηρώδης καὶ ᾿Αριστείδης
καὶ οἳ κατα᾽ τούτους τοὺς χρόνους γεγόνασι ῥήτορες. The position of
Demosthenes, Aeschines, and Isocrates outside the canon worried Lenz (pp.
53-4), who attempted to solve the matter by translating the rest of the
sentence "and the rest of the orators who have been formed together with the
three others into the group of the πραττομένη δεκάς." This is possible, but
perhaps strained; it is at least as likely that there were several lists of the first
and second generations of orators.

39. Photius, *Bibliotheca* (*Codex* 158), states that Phrynichus prescribed
Demosthenes and the "circle of nine orators"; his language may be
anachronistic, though we would expect the lexicographer to be dogmatic.

40. They are: Antiphon (7), Andocides (1), Lysias (10), Isaeus (0),
Demosthenes (40), Hyperides (14), Isocrates (12), Aeschines (0), Lycurgus
(0), Dinarchus (1).

41. Pp. 41-5. Householder's statistics cover Lucian and 13 other writers
of the imperial period. He suggested that Lucian's neglect of Lysias was the
fault of his teachers who preferred the later Attic orators over the earlier
ones. His statistics are valuable, but he does not take adequate account of
Phrynichus and the linguistic issues of the second century. Behr, pp. 11-12, n.
29, notes eight references to Lysias by Aristides; Isocrates received four
mentions and Demosthenes 28.

42. *VS*, p. 565. There is a variant on this episode on p. 539, where
Herodes is hailed at the Olympic Games as the equal of Demosthenes.

43. Philostratus, *VS*, pp. 480-84, credits Gorgias with founding the first
or older sophistic, and Aeschines the second. Extempore speaking was

Lucian was well within the critical conventions in giving priority to Demosthenes. Zeus is made to praise the orator as θαυμαστός, and is told by Hermes that imitation of the *Philippics* is the fashion of contemporary oratory.[44] He is the perfect husband of Oratory and the star pupil of Paideia.[45] His δεινότης is commended, and he recurs as a καλός orator.[46] The villain of the *Rhetorum Praeceptor* rather illogically scorns him as χαρίτων ἄμοιρος.[47] Manuscripts written in his own hand are recommended to the ignorant bibliomane as great treasures.[48] Friendly parody is a further compliment.[49] The Demosthenes question is finally summed up by Lucian in his *Demosthenis Encomium*; I have defended the authenticity of this piece elsewhere, and summarise my arguments and conclusions in a footnote.[50]

variously credited to Pericles or Python of Byzantium or Aeschines again. Philostratus' register of older sophists is: Eudoxus of Cnidus, Leon of Byzantium, Dias of Ephesus, Carneades, Philostratus the Egyptian, Theomnestus, Gorgias, Protagoras, Hippias, Prodicus, Polus, Thrasymachus, Antiphon (confused once with Antiphon the poet), Critias, Isocrates, and Aeschines. Other Attic orators receive passing mention (Demosthenes, Isaeus, Hyperides).

44. *Jupiter Tragoedus* 14.23.

45. *Bis Accusatus* 31, *Somnium* 12.

46. *De Mercede Conductis* 5.25.

47. At first blush, this is odd advice since Demosthenes is a prime influence and theme in contemporary oratory. However, Philostratus shows that themes to the discredit of Demosthenes were not uncommon, and this may be the point here. Isocrates and Plato are ridiculed by the *Rhetorum Praeceptor* in this passage, but not Aeschines; the advice is probably sectarian.

48. *Adversus Indoctum* 4.

49. E.g., in *Bis Accusatus* 26 Oratory combines the opening sentences of the *De Corona* and the *Third Olynthiac*. Zeus addresses the gods with a flourish from the *First Olynthiac*, but soon confesses that his borrowed eloquence is running out (*Jupiter Tragoedus* 15).

50. Baldwin 1969, pp. 54-62. Apart from Bauer, I seem to be alone in defending the piece. There are three traditional objections, summed up by Macleod, Loeb *Lucian*, Vol. 8, p. 237, as "its lack of inspiration, its inferior Greek and its avoidance of hiatus." These objections are not insuperable. Avoidance of hiatus may be explained as a stylistic tribute to Demosthenes who was notably careful in this regard. Helm assembled a long list of words and usages in his *RE* article which he condemned as "Sprache ganz unmöglich von Lukian." My article demonstrates that virtually all of Helm's examples are respectable Greek; in two cases (the noun δημοθοινία and the use of

The question of Lucian's personal comments on contemporary orators was earlier analysed. To the epigram on Lollianus may be added two further epigrams of equally doubtful status against the sophist Butos and Cappadocian orators in general.[51] There are a number of casual observations on sophistic practice. The gods are brought forward as literary critics more than once. Zeus ridicules the hackneyed themes of the age, and Hermes bids a rhetorician throw away his stock of technical tricks before entering Charon's boat.[52] Prologues of inordinate length are denounced, as are threnodies which are eked out by traditional details.[53] The vanity and material ambitions of orators are castigated; Lucian's own guilt in this respect is glaringly obvious.[54] The stentorian gasconade of the Cynics is a favourite theme, though the oratory of Demonax has to be allowed as a virtuous exception.[55]

The *Rhetorum Praeceptor* forms a compendium of Lucian's favourite dogmas and criticisms on the subject. He was not alone in devoting a diatribe to contemporary oratory; Aristides took a stern moral position in his abuse of sophists.[56] Lucian presents two

κελεύω with the dative), the offending usages actually occur elsewhere in Lucian. Subjective arguments are impossible to counter, but it can be saidthat the Homeric poet Thersagoras, one of the dialogue's protagonists, is a typical Lucian creation (he thinks he is divinely inspired, prays to statues for a good flow of verse, compares prose to poetry as though this procedure were a valid critical approach, and so on). The piece should be taken in the context of rhetorical exercises for and against Demosthenes; my article examines two such effusions (*P. Oxy.* 858, and *P. Oxy.* 1799). Lucian's dialogue perhaps sums up his attitude to Demosthenes as evinced in his other references. Final proof is impossible either way, but it is fair to say that the theme was an obvious one for Lucian, and perhaps balances the *Rhetorum Praeceptor*.

51. *Epigrams* 42 and 43.

52. *Jupiter Tragoedus* 32, *Dialogues of the Dead*, 10.10.

53. *Nigrinus* 10, *Timon* 37 (prologues); *De Luctu* 20.23 (threnodies). A distinction is drawn between historiographical and oratorical prologues in *De Historia conscribenda* 52-3. Lucian may have had the ostentatious grief of Herodes in mind in the *De Luctu*.

54. *Parasitus* 52 (if the piece is genuine) is a good example of this commonplace; the material ambitions of the sophists (including Lucian) need no further comment.

55. *Demonax* 4.9.

56. See Behr, pp. 106-7. *VS*, p. 585, shows that Philostratus had his doubts about the merits of this sometimes heterodox sophist.

roads to oratorical accomplishment. First comes the traditional approach of hard work and close study of Attic models (Demosthenes in particular). This advice reflects that given to Lucian by Paideia in the *Somnium*. The advocate is a muscular and bronzed fellow, a description which may be taken to fit the Syrian-born Lucian. Not that the point should be pushed, since there is an obvious contrast with the second speaker, who is epicene and elegant. The modernistic teacher is weakly handsome, with a honey-sweet voice, of mincing gait, rather bald, and soaked in perfume. He is the epitome of a Philostratean sophist. Isaeus was noted for extravagant dress; Scopelian had mellifluous tones (so, incidentally, did Pollux); Aristocles became a dandy after a slovenly period of cultivating the philosophic image; Alexander shone with his elaborate hair style and gleaming white teeth; Adrian cultivated the status symbols of ostentatious jewels and elaborate carriage.[57] He is a δαιμόνιον ἄνδρα, which recalls descriptions of Polemo and Alexander.[58] The professed scorn of culling the classics is matched in part by Polemo, who was on record as regarding the memorising of chunks of the Attic models as the most tedious of occupations; there is a contrast here with Herodes, whose capacity for study earned him the title of σιτευτὸν ῥήτορα.[59] The principal virtues of the modern orator are ignorance, audacity, effrontery, and lack of shame. These qualities are carefully selected; they are antithetical to those prescribed to Lucian by Paideia in the *Somnium*.[60] Technical prerequisites are a loud voice and the shameless μέλος style of delivery. This is associated with the ᾠδή, ascribed by Philostratus to Favorinus,

57. *VS*, p. 513 (Isaeus), p. 519 (Scopelian), p. 567 (Aristocles), p. 570 (Alexander), p. 587 (Adrian). It is notable that Philostratus claims conversion from elegance to sobriety in the case of Isaeus and from squalor to style in Aristocles; the attitude is Lucianic. The extravagances of Adrian are reported as a source of emulation in others.

58. *VS*, p. 535 (Polemo's arrogance made him treat the gods as equals), p. 570 (the godlike beauty of Alexander). The epithet is obviously commonplace, but perhaps reflects contemporary personal conceits.

59. *VS*, p. 565; Herodes is contrasted with οἱ ὀλίγωροί τε καὶ λεπτοί.

60. *Somnium* 10. The prescribed virtues are moderation, justice, piety, kindliness, reasonableness, understanding, steadfastness, love of beauty, and love of the sublime. Lucian certainly did not inherit all of these!

Dionysius of Miletus, Adrian, and Varus of Laodicea;[61] the Asianist chant is mocked elsewhere by Lucian.[62] A short selection of Attic words, seasoned by archaisms and neologisms, is commended, as is a willingness to bluster one's way through barbarisms and solecisms.[63] Stock examples from Greek history may smother defects of coherence and logic. Marathon, the Athos canal, Xerxes and the Hellespont are prime examples.[64] Useful stage effects include thigh-slapping (a technique which can be traced back to Cleon), leaping about the podium, and cries of "woe." These traits are corroborated in Philostratus, as are the ancillary techniques of insulting the audience, importing hired applause, and the cultivation of a notorious private life.[65]

Lucian combined Asianism and Atticism in his target. This was proper. Both styles competed, and sometimes fused, in his age. It might be inferred from Philostratus that Asianism began to succumb to Atticism in the second century. In fact, there was no straight line of development. Geography played a certain role. Ionia in general, Smyrna and Ephesus in particular, was the centre of Asianism. This is clear from Philostratus, who uses "Ionian"

61. *VS*, p. 491 (Favorinus), p. 513 (Dionysius), p. 589 (Adrian), p. 620 (Varus). Philostratus reports Isaeus' rebuke of Dionysius for this, and is contemptuous of Varus.

62. *Demonax* 12. The victim is Favorinus, whose anatomical deficiencies made him particularly vulnerable to this criticism. On his style see Mary C. Goggin, "Prose Rhythm in Favorinus," *Yale Class Stud* 12, 1951, pp. 149-201.

63. Recall Philostratus' anecdote concerning Philagrus, mentioned earlier.

64. Varus of Perge (nicknamed "the stork") was notorious for the Athos and Hellespont themes (*VS*, p. 576), and Ptolemy of Naucratis was dubbed "Marathon" for his excessive use of the episode (*VS*, p. 595). See *Jupiter Tragoedus* 32 for another hit at the Marathon theme.

65. Scopelian was prone to thigh slapping (*VS*, p. 519), Dionysius to cries of dismay (*VS*, p. 522), Polemo to leaping about (*VS*, p. 537), Alexander to insulting listeners (*VS*, p. 571). A lecture of Philagrus was broken up by pupils of Herodes (*VS*, p. 579), and Aristides brought in his own claque (*VS*, p. 583). Demonax was not above interrupting lectures (*Demonax* 14). The young Isaeus had been amorous and drunken (*VS*, p. 513), and Chrestus of Byzantium was fond of the bottle (*VS*, p. 591), such traits are satirised in Lucian's *Convivium*.

and "Ephesian" as synonyms for Asianist. The style was imported to Athens by practitioners such as Lollianus, and was alive in the fourth century thanks to figures like Himerius. It is also notable that a pupil did not always follow his teacher's style. Herodes marked a distinct Atticist break, and he was schooled by the most luminous representatives of Asianism. Atticism was the natural taste of the lexicographers; the hostility of Phrynichus to the diction of Lollianus is not surprising. Philostratus settled the matter long before modern scholars closed their debates,[66] by recognising the fusion of styles in the sophist Athenodorus.[67]

The evolution of Lucian's style followed the above pattern. His early activities in Ionia suggest that his training was Asianist. The point is almost proved by Oratory's claim in *Bis Accusatus* 27: καὶ κλεινὸν αὐτὸν καὶ ἀοίδιμον ἐποίουν κατακοσμοῦσα καὶ περιστέλλουσα. The related passage in *Piscator* 29 indicates that Lucian abandoned the sophistic pyrotechnics advocated by the *Rhetorum Praeceptor*: Ἐγὼ γὰρ ἐπειδὴ τάχιστα συνεῖδον ὁπόσα τοῖς ῥητορεύουσιν ἀναγκαίον τὰ δυσχερῆ προσεῖναι, ἀπάτην καὶ ψεῦδος καὶ θρασύτητα καὶ βοὴν καὶ ὠθισμοὺς καὶ μυρία ἄλλα, ταῦτα μέν, ὥσπερ εἰκὸς ἦν, ἀπέφυγον. The dissembling in the *Zeuxis*, *Bacchus*, and *Prometheus es in verbis* shows how concerned Lucian was to get the best of both worlds. He affected displeasure at being praised for his innovations because the audience was overlooking his adherence to the technical conventions of language and expression. This is in accord with *Bis Accusatus* 33, where Lucian deplores the charge of Dialogue that he has perverted him into a ξένον φάσμα by his innovations; the accusation is turned aside by appealing to Old Comedy as the legitimate precedent for the Menippus dialogues.

Lucian's views on oratory, serious or satiric, rarely depart from the conventions of the second century. Virtually every detail is corroborated by his contemporaries and by Philostratus. The point is muted by Bompaire:

66. See Bowersock, *Sophists*, pp. 9-10, for discussion and bibliography; the most notable statement is that by Wilamowitz, "Asianismus und Attizismus," *Hermes* 35, 1900, pp. 1-52.
67. *VS*, p. 594.

> Si l'on songe que le *Maître de Rhétorique* veut être la critique d'un homme de lettres, à tout le moins d'un professionnel de l'éloquence, on pourra s'étonner de la part qu'y tiennent les réflexions extra-littéraires. Leur importance n'est explicable qu'en vertu précisément d'une tradition dont les flèches sont complètement émoussées.[68]

Bompaire goes on to invoke the precedents of Archilochus and Aristophanes. The tradition is undeniable (Lucian makes no secret of his debt to Aristophanes), but the conclusion is false. The "réflexions extra-littéraires" were integral to the second sophistic. Philostratus is witness to this on nearly every page. Academic in-fighting has never been famous for its mildness of tone. The material rewards at stake in the second century made acerbity inevitable. The tone has been seen in Gellius and Phrynichus; it recurs in the Ulpian-Cynulcus clashes in Athenaeus. The fact that it was ubiquitous before and after Lucian is irrelevant. The satirist exactly reflects the tastes and behaviour of his age. Housman would have been entirely at home in the second century, but the fact of a tradition of polemic does not disqualify his abuse as contemporary criticism. Lucian did not possess the only sharp tongue in the second century, and it is a pity that we have to wait for his scholiasts before seeing him at the receiving end.

---

68. Bompaire, p. 476. Helm's Menippus fantasies are equally irrelevant; Lucian made no secret of his sources of inspiration. Incidentally, Lucian mentions Archilochus in *Pseudologistes* 2, and Hippodromus was fond of saying that Homer was the voice of the sophists but Archilochus their breath (*VS*, p. 620).

Five
Clio Dethroned

Marcus Aurelius interested himself in the principles of historiography, and perhaps dabbled in the art; he ended up by finding the study of history monotonous and depressing.[1] The reaction was possibly inevitable in one unlucky enough to have Fronto as teacher and example. His final attitude was a lonely one. Herodian remarked on the plethora of accounts of Marcus' campaigns, and was impressed by their quality.[2] We are in no position to agree or disagree with his view. Lucian likened the crop of compilers of *Parthica* to the plague of Abdera; it would be rash to accept his sarcastic critique uncritically, though if Fronto's efforts were typical, there is little cause to regret the loss of the offending monographs.

Clio was worshipped in several ways.[3] Universal history was brought up to date by Phlegon of Tralles, whom the *Historia Augusta* took to be a convenient cover for Hadrian; the dubious biographer also furnishes the imperial freedman with an historian-freedman of his own.[4] Phlegon is credited by Suidas with

1. An early letter from Fronto (Haines 1.19) mentions that Marcus had requested advice on the writing of history. *Meditations*, 3.14, has an apparent reference to some writings on Greek and Roman history, but it is not certain that they were the emperor's own work. For Marcus' views on history see Farquharson, pp. 401, 856-7.
2. Herodian 1.2; the reference is to military history, and the authors are "many and wise." *HA, Verus* 1.1, claims to know many accounts of Marcus and Verus.
3. See Bowie, pp. 10-24, for a detailed conspectus.
4. *HA, Hadrian* 16, claims that Hadrian was the real author of at least a

monographs on longevity and miracles, topics of interest to Lucian and perhaps inevitable elements in a universal historian. Another contributory factor in Marcus' disenchantment with history may have been the Roman annals of his freedman, Chryseros.[5] What little we know of his work (it covered the period from the founding of Rome to the death of Marcus Aurelius) suggests that Bowie is right to see it as an example of centering world history on Roman. This principle is firmly enunciated by Appian,[6] and was to be the inspiration of Dio Cassius and obscurer figures such as Asinius Quadratus.[7] A rival technique was to exclude Rome from account by ending world history with Alexander or the fall of Athens in 322. Practicioners of this craft included Cephalion, assigned to the reign of Hadrian by Suidas,[8] and the shadowy Jason of Argos.[9] This viewing of history from a Greek perspective is in natural accord with the preponderance of classical themes ascribed to the sophists by Philostratus. Taken together, the two techniques of writing world history evoke the conflicts of Greek intellectuals over the crucial issue of the correct attitude towards the power of Rome. Lucian himself falls sharply into this context; his own opinions will be analysed in the next chapter. A possible compromise in approach may have been attempted by Aulus Claudius Charax of Pergamum, whose 40 books of history brought Greek and Roman matters down to the reign of Nero.[10] This broader approach is obviously reminiscent of Plutarch, whose biographical efforts embraced Greeks, Romans of the Republic, and emperors. Finally, the Παντοδαπὴ Ἱστορία of Favorinus may be included here, if anywhere.

Universal history was not a universal diet. The Alexander industry was firmly established by now, and still in high gear,

---

biography of himself which was published under the names of Phlegon and other freedmen. *HA, Severus* 20.1, alludes to the writings of Aelius Maurus, freedman of Phlegon. For Phlegon himself see F. Jacoby, *FGrH*, no. 257.

  5. *FGrH*, no. 96 (and commentary, p. 300).
  6. In the Preface to his *Roman History*, especially 12-13.
  7. *FGrH*, no. 97 (and commentary, p. 301).
  8. *FGrH*, no. 93.
  9. *FGrH*, no. 94; see Bowie, p. 13, on the chronological problems.
  10. *FGrH*, no. 103; Bowie, p. 13, on the problem of Charax' title.

attracting biographers, historians, and rhetoricians. Apart from the familiar contributions of Plutarch and Dio Chrysostom, we know of the works by Potamon and Apion in the early imperial period,[11] of Amyntianus in the second century, of Criton of Pieria of uncertain date,[12] and some anonymous fragments.[13] It is worth noting that Amyntianus addressed his monograph to Marcus Aurelius; Trajan or the Severans would have been more flattered. Some contrasts between intellectual and imperial cliques may be legitimate: Marcus Aurelius, Amyntianus, and Chryseros on one side; Verus and the *Parthici* on another; Fronto straddling uneasily between the two; Lucian waxing satiric, but still keeping an eye for the main chance. Apart from Amyntianus,[14] Arrian is the obvious and central figure.[15]

Contemporary history was now in quite flourishing co-existence with the aforementioned genres, although it tended to be restricted to imperial biographies and monographs on individual wars. Plutarch had established the former category by Lucian's time, and Suetonius is naturally relevant to the theme, if not to Lucian and the majority of Greek writers. Josephus provides important evidence in more than one regard: apart from the obvious relevance of his *Jewish War*, he mentions various monographs on the civil wars of 69 and, even more to the point, berates contemporary Greeks for preferring ancient history to the great events of their own time.[16] After making due allowance for

11. *FGrH*, no. 147 (Potamon), no. 616 (Apion).

12. *FGrH*, no. 277; see Bowie, p. 14.

13. *P. Oxy* 1798 (*FGrH*, no. 148); the *fragmentum Sabbaiticum* (FGrH, no. 151).

14. According to Photius, *Bibliotheca* (*Cod.* 97a), Amyntianus also produced parallel lives of Greeks and Romans; Photius did not think much of them.

15. It is notable that Lucian makes Diogenes ridicule Alexander's claims to divinity in *Dialogues of the Dead* 13; the relationships between Alexander and historians in the *De Historia conscribenda* are reviewed from the standpoint of a Diogenes. To my earlier discussion and references on the subjects of Arrian, Alexander, and deification, add J. Tondriau, "L'avis de Lucien sur la divinisation des hommes," *Museum Helveticum* 5, 1948, pp. 124-32. Critics tend to overlook the simple fact that emperors were deified in Lucian's time; the theme was a timely one for discreet comment.

16. *BJ* 4.496; *Pref.* 1.13 (diatribe against Greeks).

his ethnic prejudices, it is clear that we are back to the aforementioned clashes of Greek intellectuals concerning what attitude to adopt to Rome.

Nearer to Lucian and the producers of *Parthica*, Arrian again stands prominent, but far from alone, Fronto was inspired by the Parthian theme. So was Polyaenus, who mentions in his *Stratege-mata* a projected work on the Parthian Wars.[17] A little earlier, Statilius Crito, a doctor of Trajan, had turned his diagnostic talents to that emperor's *Getica*;[18] it is worth noting that a doctor turns up in Lucian's gallery of hopeless historians.[19] There had also been a treatise on the Jewish war under Hadrian by Ariston of Pella.[20] And, of course, Appian is further evidence for the renewed popularity of military history.

The pursuit of imperial biography, earlier exemplified by Plutarch and Suetonius, was continued, with Hadrian the natural favourite theme.[21] Not that the various genres under discussion should be kept firmly apart. As Bowie sensibly observes, mono-graphs on particular campaigns afforded much scope for biographi-cal and encomiastic detail. So, for that matter, would universal histories. And biography was not restricted to imperial subjects. Plutarch had demonstrated the possibilities of the genre, as had Suetonius, whose biographies encompassed poets, grammarians, and famous whores as well as emperors. These traditions were to continue. Philostratus is the most obvious example; Arrian was the subject of a biography by Dio Cassius;[22] Arrian himself is credited

17. *Strat.* 8, *Pref.* (dedicated to Marcus Aurelius and Verus in 162).

18. *FGrH*, no. 200; his work is mentioned by Galen (12.445 K).

19. *De Historia conscribenda* 16. The writer in question was Callimor-phus; he perhaps got off so lightly because of Lucian's usual respect for doctors. Galen's views on his work would doubtless have been entertaining.

20. *FGrH*, no. 201.

21. A notable example may have been the biography by Philo of Byblos, on whom see Bowie, p. 16, and *FGrh*, no. 790. The generally hostile attitude of the *HA* to Hadrian may simply be perverse. However, this tone may have been exaggerated. For instance, *HA, Hadrian* 25.7, says of the emperor's obsequies "invisusque omnibus sepultus est." The epithet is commonly translated "hated," but Birley, p. 61, argues that it means "unseen." Nevertheless, in view of Hadrian's prickly relations with men of letters, a hostile attitude is explicable.

22. Attested by Suidas; its loss is regrettable.

by Lucian[23] with a biography of Tilliborus the bandit, which could have been either a straightforward and hostile account, or a parody of the genre. Hence, the wide range of biographies (or pseudo-biographies) exhibited by the *Historia Augusta* had ample precedent. Autobiography is far less attested, although Appian claims to have published one,[24] and it was always open to writers to include personal items as they thought fit.

Biographies, favourable and hostile, were well suited to sophistic practice. Lucian made use of both types. The *Demonax* and *Peregrinus* provide balance of sorts, whilst the *Alexander* provokes contrast with the genre represented by the biography of Apollonius of Tyana. The sophistic aspect has a general application to this chapter, and will be pursued later.

The enthusiasm for history in the second century evokes no surprise. The commonplace themes of the sophists were compounded of fairy tale and nostalgia. The joint popularity of Demosthenes and Alexander looks superficially perverse, but there is a discernible logic in the copulation. Alexander afforded some material for sophistic themes as well as for biographers and historians; Fronto is evidence for this as well as Philostratus.[25] He was equally a theme in real life for emperors, from the careful cultivation of the image by Trajan to the obsessional devotion of the Severans, above all Caracalla.[26] All this lent some substance to

23. *Alexander* 2.
24. *Pref.* 15. See Misch; Momigliano, p. 94; Bowersock, *Augustus*, p. 137. It may be added that there seems to have been a slackening off in the production of imperial autobiographies and military memoirs in the Antonine period, compared to the Julio-Claudian and Flavian epochs. One would have expected the sophists not to have been unduly reticent about autobiographical details, but if Lucian is anything to go by, this was not the case.
25. Fronto (Haines 2.110) was bored by a Gallic rhetorician's declamation on Macedonian debates on the death of Alexander. Gellius, *NA* 7.8, is apparently sarcastic on rhetorical comparisons between Alexander and Scipio. Alexander, Scipio, and Hannibal discuss their rival merits before Minos in Lucian, *Dialogues of the Dead* 12. It is clear from Philostratus' examples that Alexander was normally used in themes involving Athenian orators or Greek cities.
26. See Dio, 68.30, for a typical example of Trajan's devotion to the Alexander image. Niger was hailed as a new Alexander, which was one small reason for the Severan concern to take over the cliché; Dio and the *HA* are full of stories on this subject.

the sophistic preening over their relationships with emperors. Imperial power could be mitigated by their persuasions; indeed they might improve upon Demosthenes and actually influence a monarch. At the same time, few could forget that encomium was a necessary adjunct of advice. It is probable that the popularity of mock panegyrics was an intellectual safety-valve for some. When Favorinus extolled Fever or Thersites, Fronto Smoke and Dust, and Lucian the Fly, they were discreetly making mockery of a very necessary element in their lives.[27] The satirist needed patrons as much as the courtier. Lucian baited his victims without mercy, but had also to bait his hook for patrons.[28] Genuine encomium had obvious uses; not the least of these was its part in making contemporary history acceptable to the protagonists.

The *De Historia conscribenda* is a genuine contemporary document on a true-to-life theme. The Roman victory in the Parthian campaigns recalled the great days of Trajan; such scope had not been afforded in the deceptive quietude of Antoninus' reign. The resurgence of war was perhaps at odds with the idyllic picture painted in the flatulent phrases of Aelius Aristides, but it was a golden moment for patriots and encomiasts. It will have been a welcome change for many to write about, declaim upon, and read of new Roman triumphs instead of the great days of the Republic and the glory that had been Greece. One recalls the yearnings for new martial themes in Tacitus' account of the reign of Tiberius. By the same token, new glories give an impetus to the renewed study of older ones, for comparison and contrast. And contemporary rejoicings were not only for Romans. Lucian himself did not miss the chance to insert a reference to the toll of lives exacted, in his reflections on the lot of mankind,[29] but there

27. For these trifles see A. S. Pease, "Things without Honor," *CP* 21, 1926, pp. 27-42.

28. The *Harmonides* and *Scythian* are examples of appeals to patrons. It is significant that the *Apology* is addressed to the unknown Sabinus; the device may have helped to explain away the now uncomfortable *De Mercede Conductis*, which had perhaps been inspired by an unfortunate experience between Lucian and a patron. Dr. Johnson went through a similar cycle.

29. *Cataplus* 10, where the reference to the filling of Charon's ferry with wounded soldiers from "a certain war" can fairly be taken as alluding to early Roman disasters in the Parthian campaigns. There is a conventional reference

was no reason for the average Greek not to take pleasure in a defeat of the Parthians, especially since it would be a splendid opportunity to revive the theme of the Greeks and the Persians, not to mention Alexander yet again.

And so to the manufacturers of *Parthica*. Fronto is witness to the literary productions evoked by the events in question. Possible allusions to Fronto and Arrian in Lucian's pamphlet have already been examined. There is no need to question the validity of Lucian's general target and specific victims, but doubts have been cast, thus compelling some precise discussion of details later on in this chapter. Bompaire's description of the pamphlet as "un pastiche amusant de Thucydide" is not wholly untrue, but it quite fails to take account of the contemporary nature of historiography in the second century.[30] The assemblage of literary antecedents for Lucian's critical comments marshalled by Avenarius is of equally limited relevance.[31]

Lucian addressed his pamphlet to a certain Philo. This recipient is elusive, but the name is striking in the context, in view of its other more tangible bearers, and because it features elsewhere in Lucian.[32] The production of monographs on the Parthian war is compared to the plague of Abdera, which exhibited a mania for quoting from Euripides' *Andromeda* as its most distinctive symptom. Although we are probably intended to recall the plague of Athens, the jest is grimly appropriate to the real epidemic brought back from the East. Since the pamphlet appears to have been published in 165, this is either remarkable coincidence or evidence of later editorial polishing.[33] Some general reflections on the need to distinguish history from panegyric, with

to Parthian courage and military expertise in *Navigium* 33.

30. Bompaire, p. 483; see also pp. 606-7.

31. Avenarius. He provides a useful survey of modern opinions on Lucian's pamphlet, but attaches too much significance to linguistic similarities between Lucian's prescriptions and those of other critics. The book is well reviewed by Macleod in *Classical Review* 8, 1958, pp. 41-2.

32. Lycinus' interlocutor in the *Convivium* is called Philo; so is the first speaker in the debate on beauty in the doubtful *Charidemus*.

33. The ridicule of the prophetic historian (*De Historia conscribenda* 31) implies a date of 165 or 166 for the pamphlet. References to Corinth suggest that that city saw (or heard) the first publication of the piece.

the significant example of Aristobulus,[34] leads in to the dissection
of individual historians (who are, it should be noted, all located in
Ionia and Achaea).

Jacoby has extrapolated and isolated the various victims.[35] The
first offender is unnamed, like most of his colleagues, though the
reference to his native Miletus may have been an adequate clue for
Lucian's audience. The geographical allusion would be pointless if
invented; moreover, Miletus had produced the sophist Dionysius,
who was eminent under Hadrian,[36] and an historian (or sophist-
historian) could well have come from there. His sins include an
invocation to the Muses, absurd depreciation of the Parthians, and
inept comparisons between the Roman general and Achilles and
the enemy's monarch to Thersites.[37]

The second victim is Crepereius Calpurnianus of Pompeiopolis,
whose crude imitations of Thucydides rather resemble bad
undergraduate pastiche. Both nomenclature and origin are of
interest. Various Crepereii rose to military and civilian eminences
in the imperial period.[38] A Calpurnianus was a distinguished legal
man in Egypt under Antoninus Pius;[39] another bearer of the name
received a versified treatise on denticare from Apuleius, despite (or
because of) which he later showed his teeth as one of Apuleius'
enemies.[40] Pompeiopolis was a city in Paphlagonia; it produced the

34. This was discussed earlier in the context of Lucian and Arrian. Also
relevant is *De Historia conscribenda* 38, where the historian's duty to blame
Alexander for the murder of Cleitus is insisted upon; this is contrary to
Arrian, who attempts to mitigate Alexander's guilt.

35. *FGrH*, 203; see also Homeyer.

36. Philostratus, *VS*, p. 522.

37. Fronto's comparison of Verus to Achilles has already been noted; it
could obviously have been a common conceit. Lucian breaks his own rule by
using the Thersites comparison in *Adversus Indoctum* 7. Favorinus (see
Gellius, *NA* 17.12) was not the only one to issue an adoxographical
encomium on the subject; by contrast, Quintilian, 3.7.19, makes the
unsurprising statement that Thersites was a typical theme for vituperation.
Demonax 61 praises Thersites, perhaps ironically, as a good mob orator in the
Cynic style.

38. *PIR*[2], C, 1567-74; Lucian's character is no. 1568.

39. *PIR*[2], C, no. 238.

40. Apuleius, *Apol.* 6, 60.

consular friend of Galen (perhaps also of Fronto), Cn. Claudius
Severus, who was also connected with the sophist Adrian of
Tyre.[41] Lucian's victim cannot be precisely identified, but his
names and origin are suitably evocative in context. He compounded his major vice by inserting a large number of Latin
technicalities for military machines. The phenomenon is attested
in later style, and the reverse process hardly needs comment; it is
balanced in the pamphlet by the Atticist who translated Latin
proper names into Greek. It may cautiously be subjoined that, if
Lucian's historian was in any way connected with attested
Crepereii of military distinction, his interest in Latin military
technicalities is natural enough. Finally, it is congenial, if not
significant, to find an actual general by the name of Thucydides
distinguishing himself in Dio's account of the war.[42]

Next is the medical man, Callimorphus. He wins a backhanded
compliment for having cleared the way for a real historian, but his
fragile Ionic style and frigid preface on the peculiar virtues of
doctor-historians receive crushing indictment.[43] Trajan's doctor,
Statilius Crito, has already been mentioned as an example of the
latter breed. Callimorphus' attempts to write Ionic may be seen in
the context of Galen's disdain for Atticising style. Stein[44] was
disposed to taking Callimorphus as a *nomen fictum*, although no
doubts are expressed about the other three historians named by
Lucian. There might have been grounds for suspicion if Lucian
had used the name for punning or other comic purposes, which he
does not. Names such as Callidromus are attested, and there is no
reason to expel Callimorphus.

A philosopher-historian from Corinth is unnamed. His love of
syllogism, his beard, and his vanity mark him as the typical
Lucianic butt (the same stereotype is found more than once in
Aulus Gellius). His other besetting vice is flattery. This may be
more notable than it sounds; Lucian's prefatory remarks, and
subsequent reflections, indicate that servile eulogy was the sin
most to be avoided, but the philosopher is the only historian

41. See Bowersock, *Sophists*, p. 83.
42. Dio, 71.3; the general receives a good press.
43. See earlier for the relevance of poor Ionic style to Arrian.
44. *PIR*[2], C, no. 228.

singled out on this score. His location in Corinth is not very helpful as a clue to his identity. It does not make him a native of that city, and Corinth seems not to have produced many big literary names in the period. However, in spite of the proverbial impossibility of all men going to Corinth, the city was visited by Galen, and adorned with a theatre by Herodes Atticus. Lucian's butt could have been just another visitor. Yet it is relevant to note that Corinth exhibited the aristocratic L. Gellius Menander, to whom Arrian dedicated his Epictetus discourses.[45]

Brief mention is accorded to an imitation of an imitation. Two extracts from an anonymous exordium reveal the author as not only a poor man's Herodotus (he affects Ionic style), but a poor man's Crepereius as well.

Next in line is ἄλλος τις ἀοίδιμος ἐπὶ λόγων δυνάμει, whose claims to represent Fronto have already been assessed. His elaborate portrayals of trivia, his gory details, and preposterous casualty figures are exemplified. He was also the extreme Atticist who translated or transliterated Latin proper names into Greek.[46]

The critique diverges briefly into general scorn of excessively poetic language, grossly inflated prefaces, and histories which have no preface at all. A more personal note is resumed with the ridicule of an anonymous bungler whose efforts at Thucydidean style were ruined by his geographical ignorance and mania for suicide scenes and turgid speeches.[47] A final compendium includes writers who have no ability to distinguish cardinal events from trivia, a fraudulent Corinthian (unlike the aforementioned philosopher, this man is identified as a native of Corinth) who manufactured eye-witness accounts of events he never saw, a master of breviloquence (his name is Antiochianus) whose title almost surpassed his monograph in length, and a prophet who is

45. Bowersock, *Sophists*, p. 113.
46. Fronto is not likely to have been guilty of all the vices stigmatised here by Lucian, though the ruins of the *Principia Historiae* do not allow a clear view of his work. Lucian's comments may be intended to cover Fronto and imitators or disciples.
47. This is the wretch who transplanted Lucian's native Samosata. In spite of the tradition of including speeches in histories, the technique here smacks of sophistic production.

already at work on events of the future. One final name, partially protected by a lacuna in the manuscript, is Demetrius of Sagalassus, whose title *Parthonicica* was not approved by Lucian.

Nothing can be established about any of the above. It may, however, be worth pointing out that Antiochianus recalls the sophist Antiochus of Aegae, whose Ἰστορία is commended, for its language and thought, as the best of his productions by Philostratus.[48] Antiochus was a pupil of Dionysius of Miletus. Could Lucian be alluding to this sophist (whose addiction to dreams and Aesculapius the satirist would have scorned), or a follower of his? The most pertinent Demetrius of whom we know anything is the doctor of Marcus Aurelius; he expired in 167 or 168 in the Marcomannic campaigns.[49] This man has been recently equated with the sophist Aelius Demetrius of Alexandria, but the identification is not certain,[50] and another doctor-historian (or doctor-sophist) would not be out of place in Lucian's pamphlet.

These historians form a fairly standard collection of Lucianic victims. One unusual aspect is the relative absence of personal abuse. There are no entertainingly scabrous anecdotes, and only the servile philosopher and the fabricator of eye-witness accounts are roughly handled on this level. Both victims are associated with Corinth, which may support the view that Lucian's pamphlet was first aired in that city. Another detail of note is that the four historians named are all identified by citation of their titles or preambles. Lucian perhaps wanted to single out those who had actually published part or all of their work, in Corinth or elsewhere, and isolate them from his less specific attacks which concerned general principles as much as individual cases. The majority of his comments bear upon the stylistic deficiencies of the historians, although the issue of flattery and one or two technical defects of historiographical approach are included.

Such emphasis comes naturally from Lucian; he was no profound critic, and it was usually easier to wring laughter from

48. *VS*, p. 570.
49. Galen, 14.4 K.
50. For the equation, Bowersock, *Sophists*, p. 12, p. 63; against, Stein, *PIR*[2], D, no. 44.

animadversions on style than from deep discussions of principles. Yet it may have to be admitted that the two parts of his pamphlet do not cohere very precisely. He prefaces his dissection of the historians, and concludes his register of historiographical virtues, by likening himself and his criticism to Diogenes. The device strengthens the ethical side of the arguments. Furthermore, great stress is placed on the issue of flattery in the didactic section of the monograph. But it has been seen that only the Corinthian philosopher was flagrantly guilty of servility.

It might be inferred that we are dealing with sophistic performers rather than historians proper. It seems certain that the writers were giving readings of at least extracts from their works in epideictic displays to audiences. This conclusion adds point to Lucian's initial conceit of the Abderite plague, and to his expressed desire not to be μόνος ἄφωνος ἐν οὕτω πολυφώνῳ τῷ καιρῷ; it also fits his own role of Diogenes, who had the galling habit of interrupting lectures (so, we remember, did Demonax). The recitation of panegyrics would hardly need mentioning, were it not for the relevant exasperation of Marcus Aurelius with such performances in Naples.[51] Lucian takes some pains to stress the difference between sophistic display and historiographical technique in his detailed comments on form, content, and the correct construction of a preface.[52]

"Again and again disciplines intertwine, and throughout is the prospect of public advancement." This observation by Bowersock[53] is very much to the point. Intellectual life was for the most part bilingual, versatile, and not at all enclosed in ivory towers. Versatility is the key point in our present discussion. Appian was a court pleader at Rome; Cephalion is dubbed as *rhetor* as well as historian by Suidas; Antiochus of Aegae has

51. "Encomiographos istic audiimus, Graecos scilicet sed miros mortales" (Haines 1.142). There is a reference to the popularity of panegyrics in *Charidemus* 2.

52. See earlier for Lucian's views on prefaces. The issue was an old one; Ephorus' use of prefaces was censured by Diodorus, and Polybius thought little of Hellenistic prefaces. See, e.g., Barker, pp. 68-83, and Avenarius, pp. 113-18.

53. *Sophists*, 113.

already been adduced as a history-writing sophist; in the next generation came Aelius Antipater of Hierapolis, a pupil of Adrian and Pollux, who wrote a biography of Septimius Severus.[54] The tradition of versatility was not, of course, created in the Antonine and Severan periods. Potamon, Apion, Josephus, Dio, and Plutarch are obvious examples from earlier generations.

Lucian's targets are located in Ionia and Achaea, established centres of sophistic practice. His love of twitting sophists has been earlier analysed, and demands no further comment. However, the fact that he is inspired by the writers of *Parthica* may suggest that he is mocking what were, at least in part, sophistic confections. For his age, relatively replete with historians, was not rich in theoreticians of historiography. This dearth is not to be presumed a bad thing, for our own age has sometimes tended to get bogged down in theories about history rather than get on with the job of writing history. The caustic comment of G. R. Elton[55] is very much to the point: "Every new number of *History and Theory* is liable to contain yet another article struggling to give history a philosophic basis, and some of them are interesting. But they do not, I fear, advance the writing of history." This aspect of the matter will recur later on. Meanwhile, it may be added that Aulus Gellius was inspired (if that is the right word, in view of the mess he made of his project) to compile a survey of Greek and Roman history in the form of a long string of mini-biographies, by an alleged error of chronology made in a public reading or declamation by an "ignorant sophist."[56] Gellius, in spite of his intimacy with men such as Favorinus, Fronto, and Herodes Atticus, displays a fondness for tilting at sophists in his *Noctes Atticae*.[57] And the recurring quarrels involving himself, his mentors, and both philosophers and *grammatici*, which adorn his compendium, give off a distinctly Lucianic flavour.

54. Philostratus, *VS*, p. 607; he refers to many writers of history flourishing in this period.
55. Elton, p. viii, note 1.
56. *NA* 17.21.
57. *NA* 5.3.7; 17.5.3; 17.12.1. Apart from Favorinus, the only oratorical luminary in the register of Philostratus to be named by Gellius is Herodes Atticus.

Thus, at least some of Lucian's butts might be regarded as sophistic performers. His philosopher can also be brought into the contemporary context. History and philosophy cohere most notably in the case of Arrian, a copulation clearly befitting "the new Xenophon." Not that philosophers were all on one side in the Antonine period. One side of the coin shows the successful Arrian, not to mention Marcus Aurelius and the "philosophic establishment" which so goaded Avidius Cassius. The reverse side displays the hispid agitators so regularly abused by Lucian, Aulus Gellius, and, on one occasion, by Appian.[58]

A precise distinction between genres cannot, then, be harped upon. It is not unsafe to assume that these *Parthica*, however we might wish to classify them, enjoyed some currency as historical monographs. Set aside Fronto and Arrian, and the authors owe their dubious immortality to Lucian only. It is possible that they were used by Dio, Herodian, and the *Historia Augusta*. They are nowhere honoured with a direct mention, but Herodian and the *Historia Augusta* both mention the large number of accounts of the reign of Marcus and Verus. One example shows how far speculation may or may not go. Lucian twice complains of historians who compress important events into absurdly brief compass to make room for their obsessional trivia. There is a perfect example of this in the *Historia Augusta*, where the Eastern campaigns of Avidius Cassius are compressed into half a sentence; the biographers' concern for trivia needs no comment.[59]

Lucian's prescriptions for writing good history seem for the most part conventional. Thucydides is held up as the prime model. Xenophon receives an honourable mention; Herodotus' preface is commended, but otherwise the latter is played down.[60] The

---

58. See Bowie, p. 12, note 28, for Appian's abuse of philosophers; one will obviously bear in mind Tacitus' views on Flavian philosophers.

59. *HA, Avidius Cassius* 6.5: "In Armenia et in Arabia et in Aegypto res optime gessit." Since it is increasingly hazardous to cite the *HA* as evidence for anything, I had better state that I am aware of the extreme conclusions of Syme's *Ammianus*, and *Emperors*, but prefer the more moderate views of Birley, pp. 312-14.

60. *De Historia conscribenda* 42 approves Thucydides' implied criticisms of Herodotus. Fronto (Haines 1.42) was charmed by Herodotus' style.

supreme qualities are σύνεσις πολιτική and δύναμις ἑρμηνευτική. The first of these, described as an "unteachable natural gift," baffled Avenarius in his eternal quest for literary antecedents; the term is actually Aristotelian.[61] It is no insult to Lucian to begin by detailing his rules in a simple list. The aforementioned qualities are followed by these prescriptions: military experience and expertise; avoidance of flattery; lucid expression and sober style; coherent structure; impartiality in accepting or rejecting evidence; strict adherence to the facts as received; a two-point preface expressing the nature of cause and effect; avoidance of trivial detail; a concern to make speeches fit the character of the speaker; an agnostic approach to myths, which may be retailed but not believed. The historian should aspire to win the accolade of "a free man, full of frankness, quite removed from flattery and servility, truthful in all respects."[62]

Now, much, if not all, of this will appear to be hackneyed and predictable, a superficial ragbag of prescriptions from his predecessors, teachers, and other of his own writings. On this last point, for example, it is easy to observe that frankness is a natural recommendation from one who used the dramatic *persona* Parresiades in the *Piscator*; clarity of style is a virtue urged upon Lexiphanes (and, as was earlier seen, a quality enjoined by Galen); and so on.

In fact, attitudes towards the originality of Lucian's ideas have varied considerably.[63] Wilamowitz accused him of sinking into commonplaces; Sommerbrodt and Schmid praised his originality and Thucydidean spirit. His sources have been traced to the Isocratean school of historians, or to Peripatetic theories such as the lost treatise of Theophrastus on historiography. Against this last, Avenarius points out that Cicero[64] states quite explicitly that he knew of no monographs on historiography;[65] for Avenarius,

61. Avenarius, p. 31, confesses that "habe ich in der von mir eingesehenen antiken Literatur keine ausgesprochene Parallele gefunden." The phrase occurs in Aristotle, *Politics* 1291a; its meaning is clear.

62. *De Historia Conscribenda* 61.

63. See Macleod's review for a conspectus; also Grube, p. 336.

64. *De Or.* 2.62.

65. The theory is that of Wehrli.

Lucian's treatise is not original, though above the general level of the age. Lucian will have used a variety of sources, in particular, perhaps, the lost work πῶς κρίνομεν τὴν ἀληθῆ ἱστορίαν by Plutarch, and also the ideas of his own teachers. High praise is bestowed on Lucian by Grube,[66] who calls his pamphlet "his most important critical work ... the fullest treatment of the subject since Polybius three centuries before ... the fullest discussion of historiography as a literary genre from antiquity ... Lucian's common sense makes a real contribution to literary theory."

A connection between Lucian and Polybius is striking, since this historian is nowhere adduced in the satirist's pamphlet as a model, and indeed is almost completely ignored in the entire Lucianic corpus.[67] This neglect seems typical of the age.[68] Which is not to say that Lucian never read him, or heard of him from his teachers. A malicious critic might be tempted to say that Polybius is suppressed by Lucian in order to conceal his critical debts.

A panorama of pre-Lucianic comments on historiography is not fearsomely difficult to construct; Avenarius is testimony to that! One aspect merits some special consideration for its relevance to the Antonine age and the relationship between historiography and sophistic practice. Lucian dwells on the need to separate the elements of truth and entertainment.[69] This concept bears on many genres: sophistic declamation, history of all types, and biography are especially to the point.

The self-avowed aim of Herodotus had been to chronicle the deeds of Greeks and non-Greeks; the latter get their meed of praise (as it were) when appropriate. It is notable that the very first writer in Lucian's gallery (the one who began with an invocation to the Muses) is criticised for beginning his narrative by dubbing Vologesus "an accursed rogue." Also germane is the fact that Cephalion's world history, previously discussed, aped Herodotus

66. Grube, pp. 336-38.

67. *Octogenarians* 22; an ignorant Greek called Polybius is mocked at *Demonax* 40 (not the historian, of course).

68. He is not mentioned in the extant portions of Fronto; Gellius has one cursory reference (*NA* 6.14.10). Polybius, of course, was not convenient for sophistic themes.

69. *De Historia conscribenda* 9.

by its Ionic dialect and division into nine books titled after the
Muses. Thucydides' aversion to the romantic element in history is
all too familiar. Polybius tended to wobble in his views.[70] His
general introduction agrees with his predecessors that knowledge
of the past is the best corrective for human nature. History is the
best way to the "true life." Statesmen will benefit from his
discussions on causes and effects; the layman should profit from
moral lessons afforded. The twin division into the pleasurable and
the useful is admitted; Polybius prefers the latter, but does not
altogether eschew the former. Diodorus Siculus was equally
flexible. At one time, he will define historiography as the
"mother-city of philosophy"; at another, he allows that the
pleasurable has a legitimate function.[71] Another critic, perhaps the
worst judge of historical writing produced by the ancient world,
who never worked out fully the relationship between entertainment and truth was Dionysius of Halicarnassus. For him, truth was
the proper pursuit of the historian, but this must be approached
through the selection of a proper subject. This concept dominates
his ridiculous critique of Thucydides, who stands condemned for
electing to write about the downfall of his own city.[72]

No need to multiply examples. A few words on the Roman
side will add to the picture. The fact that it is unlikely that Lucian
was well-read in Latin literature does not make the issue irrelevant.
Greek intellectuals perhaps knew more about Roman literature
than they formally acknowledged in their own productions. Aulus
Gellius[73] is witness to the fact that some salons debated the rival
merits of Greek and Latin poetry, and there is no reason to
suppose that Lucian never heard any lecture or seminar on Latin
topics.

Livy finds space in his preface for a discussion of the practical
side to historiography.[74] Tacitean claims to objectivity require
neither documentation nor comment. Innumerable definitions of

70. For this and what follows see Walbank, pp. 6-16.
71. 1.2.2; 1.2.7.
72. *Ep. ad Pomp.* 104; Bonner.
73. *NA* 19.9.
74. *Pref.* 10.

history, such as Cicero's *magistra vitae*,[75] may well afford linguistic parallels, specious or otherwise, to Lucian's comments. Transition (no big one) from the discussion of truth and entertainment to the other key issue in Lucian's treatise, namely flattery, is provided by Cicero's notorious letter to Lucceius[76] asking for an inflated account of his consulship; also by the letter of Pliny to Titinius Capito on the subject of writing history.[77] This latter piece, penned by a man whose uncle, Pliny the Elder, and close colleague and friend, Tacitus, were both historians, is of signal interest. Titinius is not the first man to urge Pliny to historiography. Pliny likes the idea, though doubts his own competence (wisely, in view of what is to come). Unlike the more exacting genres of oratory and poetry, history "gives pleasure, no matter how it is written." History may have much in common with oratory, but the two also differ sharply. Profound truth and glorious deeds are the aims of history, and the genres require different styles. And what sort of history should Pliny write? Ancient history has "been done," and it requires too much research. Contemporary history would be a more pioneer field. But: *graves offensae, levis gratia*.

This brings us back to Lucian and his age in two regards. Lucian himself had no particular interest in writing history; indeed, he specifically disavows the ambition.[78] His other allusions to the Greek historians are desultory.[79] He might be called an occasional writer of historical novelettes, and the *Vera Historia* may have been in some sense a parody of Herodotus, or of the contemporary relish for *mirabilia*.[80] History was to him, very

75. *De Or.* 2.36; see Avenarius, p. 25.
76. *Ad Fam.* 5.12.
77. *Ep.* 5.8.
78. *De Historia conscribenda* 4; the statement is, of course, partly rhetorical. Or is it a case of "those who can't, teach"?
79. Thucydides hardly occurs outside the pamphlet, apart from the reference to Demosthenes' alleged transcripts of his work in *Adversus Indoctum* 4. Allusions to Xenophon (*Somnium* 17, *Octogenarians* 21) show no interest in his actual work. Herodotus is only a handy peg for the main theme in the *Herodotus*; his alleged mendacities are adduced in *Philopseudes* 2, and they were responsible for his infernal punishment in *Vera Historia* 2.31 (he is neatly exiled along with Ctesias).
80. Photius, *Bibliotheca* (*Cod.* 166) regarded the marvellous tales of

often, little more than a convenient vehicle for literary adornment of his critical writings. He shared the sophistic nostalgia for ancient Greece, but like his contemporaries was usually ready to come to terms with the realities of the second century.

But clichés can still be striking at the right moment. The advice tendered to Fronto by Verus on the composition of *Parthica* demonstrates that Lucian's platitudes were timely.[81] The

Antonius Diogenes as Lucian's inspiration. An attempt to gather the sources was made by Stengel. Gellius, *NA* 9.4, bought a collection of second hand books of *mirabilia* by Aristeas of Proconnesus, Isigonus of Nicaea, Ctesias, Onesicritus, Philostephanus, and Hegesias. Phlegon is further evidence for the genre, as is Lucian's *Philopseudes*. Herodotus' presence in the *Philopseudes* and *Vera Historia* may hint at Lucian's intentions, but the joke is too obvious to prove anything. The *Toxaris* and *Anacharsis* might be termed novelettes, but such a label is perhaps anachronistic. However, the Greek novel offered scope for satirical treatment; see B. P. Reardon, "The Greek Novel," *Phoenix* 23, 1969, pp. 291-309, for the literature on this subject, and p. 304 for Lucian's comic approach.

81.   Verus was as blunt in stating his wishes to Fronto as Cicero had been to Lucceius (Haines 2.194-6): "Ea vero quae post meam profectionem gesta sunt ex litteris ad me scriptis a negotio cuique praepositis ducibus cognosces. Earum exemplaria Sallustius noster, nunc Fulvianus, dabit. Ego vero, ut et consiliorum meorum rationes commemorare possis, meas quoque litteras, quibus quidquid gerendum esset demonstratur, mittam tibi. Quodsi picturas quoque quasdam desideraveris, poteris a Fulviano accipere. Et quidem quo magis te quasi in rem praesentem inducerem, mandavi Cassio Avidio Martioque Vero commentarios quosdam mihi facerent, quos tibi mittam, et quibus mores hominum et sensum eorum cognosces. Quodsi me quoque voles aliquem commentarium facere, designa mihi qualem velis faciam, et ut iubes faciam. Quidvis enim subire paratus sum, dum a te res nostrae illustrentur. Plane non contempseris et orationes ad senatum et adlocutiones nostras ad exercitum. Mittam tibi et sermones meos cum barbaris habitos. Multum haec tibi conferent.

"Unam rem volo non quidem demonstrare discipulus magistro, sed existimandam dare. Circa causas et initia belli diu commoraberis, et etiam ea quae nobis absentibus male gesta sunt. Tarde ad nostra venies. Porro necessarium puto, quanto ante meum adventum superiores Parthi fuerint, dilucere, ut quantum nos egerimus appareat. An igitur debeas, quomodo πεντηκονταετίαν θουκυδίδης explicuit, illa omnia corripere, an vero paulo altius dicere, nec tamen ita ut mox nostra dispandere, ipse dispicies.

"In summa meae res gestae tantae sunt, quantae sunt scilicet, quoiquoimodi sunt: tantae autem videbuntur, quantas tu eas videri voles."

issue of flattery was as practical as it was ethical. For historians as well as sophists (not forgetting the aforementioned possible combination of the two roles) were adept at rising to high positions. Arrian enjoyed a consulship, a military command, and a provincial governorship; Appian gained a procuratorial position under Antoninus Pius; Aulus Claudius Charax was consul in 147, and a provincial governor;[82] Antiochus of Aegae eschewed offices himself, but his descendants were consuls; Phlegon and Chryseros were imperial freedmen, Statilius Crito a royal doctor. And this trend continued into the next generations. Witness Galen, Dio Cassius, and Aelius Antipater, the last of whom moved through the ranks of imperial secretary, consul, and governor of Bithynia until removed from this last office for his sanguinary exercise of authority.[83]

Hence, the writers of *Parthica* had more to hope for from their productions than mere literary fame. The career of Lucian never reached the exalted heights of the above examples. A double conclusion has to be reached on the merits and purpose of his pamphlet. It is true that Lucian wrote within a series of conventions, though a monograph on historiography was perhaps a relative rarity for the ancient world. However, these conventions could be adapted by the writers of the second century to their own circumstances. Lucian's treatise has a contemporary sting which Avenarius and Bompaire are not willing enough to concede. Historiography was a real topic of the age, and excited Lucian's usual combination of personal criticism and intellectual dogmatism. Without this contemporary stimulus, he would not have written the *De Historia Conscribenda*.

But we must also reckon with Lucian the careerist. He nowhere takes the historians to task for undue magnification of Verus, and does not try to deflate the military achievement of Rome and her generals. His prescriptions on the general ethics of

82. See Bowie, p. 13, and Bowersock, *Sophists*, p. 113, on Charax. The efforts of Fronto advanced Appian under Antoninus; it is clear from the careful tone of his letter (Haines 1.262) that the emperor had not been in a hurry to advance the historian. Perhaps this is why Appian repaid part of his debt by his aforementioned abuse of philosophers.

83. Philostratus, *VS*, p. 607.

flattery and stylistic matters were carefully phrased, and not likely to get him into any trouble with eminent men. In view of his *Imagines* and the possible connection with Verus (discussed in an earlier chapter), this was prudent. What, one wonders, would Lucian have done if approached by Verus or a general for a suitable monograph on their exploits? Some may feel that Lucian's later *Apology* provides the answer.

Six
Gods and Men

Byzantine commentators took it into their heads that Lucian was the Anti-Christ; we have seen that the notion was pervasive down to the eighteenth century.[1] Then the fashion was adapted to the changed intellectual climate of Europe, and by a natural transition the satanic label was exchanged for favourable comparisons with Voltaire.[2] The present century has brought about another change in Lucian's reputation. He is now presented as an antiquarian flogger of dead horses, a satirist whose work was set in a study, not in the real life of the second century. Thus, the often judicious Caster could conclude that "son ambition n'était pas de peindre spécialement son temps, comme un Juvenal."[3] Perhaps the most crushing indictment is registered by Highet: "When I try to read those satires in which, with the same subtlety as a freshman preaching atheism, he deflates the ancient Bronze-Age myths of Zeus and the Olympians and lards his thin dictionary-Attic prose with cultured quotations from the correct classics, I feel as though I were trying to savor a satire on the medieval Christian cult of relics, written in Chaucerian verse by an intelligent Hindu of the present day. To put it bluntly, most of Lucian's problems are dead, and were dead when he wrote about them; his language is a colorless pastiche; and he has almost wholly abandoned one of the

1. See my first chapter and surveys such as Förster.
2. This conceit is documented by Allinson, *Lucian*, pp. 170-73. The approach is exemplified by J. W. Hewitt, "A Second century Voltaire," *CJ* 20, 1924, pp. 132-42.
3. Caster, *Lucien*, p. 388.

essential virtues of satire, which is to be topical in subject and realistic, urgent, combative in style."[4]

If satirists are allowed to follow their trade in Hades, Lucian has been provided with ample material for at least a *Tris Accusatus*. The Anti-Christ label is the easiest to detach. It may be a matter for relief or regret, but Lucian was one of the least qualified candidates for the position of adjutant to Satan. The problem is not to demonstrate his unsuitability, but to trace the evolution of the myth.

Prior to the Suidas "biography," there is no hint of the tradition. Brief *testimonia* are provided by Eunapius, Lactantius, and Isidore of Pelusium; these are supplemented by Photius' discussion of the satirist.

1. Λουκιανὸς δὲ ὁ ἐκ Σαμοσάτων, ἀνὴρ σπουδαῖος ἐς τὸ γελασθῆναι, Δημώνακτος φιλοσόφου κατ᾿ ἐκείνους τοὺς χρόνους βίον ἀνέγραψεν, ἐν ἐκείνῳ τε τῷ βιβλίῳ καὶ ἄλλοις ἐλαχίστοις δι᾿ ὅλου σπουδάσας.

(Eunapius, *VS*, p. 454)

2. "Lucianus, qui diis et hominibus non pepercit."

(Lactantius, *Inst. Div.*, I. 9)

3. Παρὰ τῶν Κυνικῶν, ὧν εἷς ἦν καὶ Λουκιανός, ὁ τοὺς διαλόγους κατὰ πάντων ὁμοῦ σχεδὸν τῶν τε εἰρημένων, τῶν τε παραλελειμμένων, συντάξας.   (Isidore, *Epistulae* IV. 55)

4.   Ἀνεγνώσθη Λουκιανοῦ ὑπὲρ φαλάριδος καὶ νεκρικοὶ καὶ ἑταιρικοὶ διάλογοι διάφοροι, καὶ ἕτεροι διαφόρων ὑποθέσεων λόγοι, ἐν οἷς σχεδὸν ἅπασι τὰ τῶν Ἑλλήνων κωμῳδεῖ, τήν τε τῆς θεοπλαστίας αὐτῶν πλάνην καὶ μωρίαν καὶ τὴν εἰς ἀσέλγειαν ἄσχετον ὁρμὴν καὶ ἀκρασίαν, καὶ τῶν ποιητῶν αὐτῶν τὰς τερατώδεις δόξας καὶ ἀναπλάσεις, καὶ τὸν ἐντεῦθεν πλάνον τῆς πολιτεάς, καὶ τοῦ ἄλλου βίου τὴν ἀνώμαλον περιφορὰν καὶ τὰς περιπτώσεις, καὶ τῶν φιλοσόφων αὐτῶν τὸ φιλόκομπον ἦθος καὶ μηδὲν ἄλλο πλὴν ὑποκρίσεως καὶ κενῶν δοξασμάτων μεστόν· καὶ ἁπλῶς, ὡς ἔφημεν, κωμῳδία τῶν Ἑλλήνων ἐστὶν αὐτῷ ἡ σπουδὴ ἐν λόγῳ πεζῷ. Ἔοικε δὲ αὐτὸς τῶν μηδὲν ὅλως πρεσβευόντων εἶναι· τὰς γὰρ ἄλλων κωμῳδῶν καὶ διαπαίζων δόξας, αὐτὸς ἦν θειάζει οὐ τίθησι, πλὴν εἴ τις αὐτοῦ δόξαν ἐρεῖ τὸ μηδὲν δοξάζειν. Τὴν

---

4. Highet, *Satire*, pp. 42-3; he goes on to throw a few crumbs of praise to Lucian for the *Rhetorum Praeceptor, Adversus Indoctum*, and *De Mercede Conductis*.

μέντοι φράσιν ἐστὶν ἄριστος, λέξει εὐσήμῳ τε καὶ κυρίᾳ καὶ τῷ
ἐμφατικῷ διαπρεπούσῃ κεχρημένος, εὐκρινείας τε καὶ καθαρότητος
μετά γε τοῦ λαμπροῦ καὶ συμμέτρου μεγέθους, εἴ τις ἄλλος ἐραστής.
Συνθήκη τε αὐτῷ οὕτως ἥρμοσται ὥστε δοκεῖν τὸν ἀναγινώσκοντα
μὴ λόγους λέγειν, ἀλλὰ μέλος τι τερπνὸν χωρὶς ἐμφανοῦς ᾠδῆς τοῖς
ὠσὶν ἐναποστάζειν τῶν ἀκροατῶν. Καὶ ὅλως, ὥσπερ ἔφημεν,
ἄριστος ὁ λόγος αὐτῷ καὶ οὐ πρέπων ὑποθέσεσιν, ἃς αὐτὸς ἔγνω συν
τῷ γελοίῳ διαπαῖξαι. Ὅτι δὲ αὐτὸς τῶν μηδὲν ἦν ὅλως δοξαζόντων,
καὶ τὸ τῆς βίβλου ἐπίγραμμα δίδωσιν ὑπολαμβάνειν. Ἔχει γὰρ ὧδε·
        Λουκιανὸς τάδ᾽ ἔγραψα, παλαιά τε μωρά τε εἰδώς·
        μωρὰ γὰρ ἀνθρώποις καὶ τὰ δοκοῦντα σοφά,
        κοὐδὲν ἐν ἀνθρώποισι διακριδόν ἐστι νόημα·
        ἀλλ᾽ ὃ σὺ θαυμάζεις, τοῦθ᾽ ἑτέροισι γέλως.
                                    (Photius, Bibliotheca (Cod. 128)

Eunapius' comment is placed in his general preamble, in which
he plays that most professorial of games and justifies his own book
by criticising the deficiencies of his predecessors in the field. His
attitude to Philostratus is patronising,[5] and the inclusion of Lucian
might be taken as an implied rebuke for his omission by the earlier
biographer. Eunapius was forthrightly anti-Christian, and his
failure to adduce or defend Lucian in this context is perhaps
significant. His view of Lucian as a serious satirist is unremarkable;
however, we would like to know those works other than the
Demonax which were considered by him to be wholly serious.

The mild testimony of Lactantius and Isidore is striking. The
former was not usually afraid to call a spade a shovel, and it seems
impossible that he knew of any Anti-Christ tradition concerning
Lucian. Isidore's definition of Lucian as a cynic was a natural
inference from the Diogenes and Menippus elements in the
satirist's work, and especially if he took the Cynicus to be
genuine.[6]

5. Eunapius, VS, p. 454: φιλόστρατος μὲν ὁ Λήμνιος τοὺς τῶν ἀρίστων
σοφιστῶν ἐξ ἐπιδρομῆς μετὰ χάριτος παρέπτυσε βίους, φιλοσόφων δὲ οὐδεὶς
ἀκριβῶς ἀνέγραψεν·
6. The Isidore letter is to Harpocras the Sophist (text in Migne, PG,
LXXVIII). The main objections to the Cynicus are its stylistic features (rarely
conclusive) and the confounding of Lycinus by his Cynic opponent. See
Macleod, Loeb Lucian, Vol. 8, p. 379, for discussion of the matter; the piece
has been assigned to the reign of Julian, but there is no evidence for anything
conclusive.

The more expansive comments of Photius indicate a belief in Lucian's atheism, but the Patriarch found no difficulty in praising him as a serious critic of pagan philosophy and religion. Not many critics would join him in singling out the *Phalaris* as a representative piece, but it is pleasant to visualise Photius reading through the *Dialogues of the Courtesans*. These latter, as has been seen, did not shock him as did the *Asinus*.[7] Elsewhere, he discusses the *Vera Historia*; this is predictable, since Photius had a weakness for the novel except when "obscene" matter intruded.[8] His failure to condemn Lucian as a notorious anti-Christian is notable, for he is rarely unwilling to stigmatise the impious and the heretics.[9]

In view of the above evidence, the strident tone of Suidas comes as a shock. The problem is compounded by the difficulty inherent in accepting Hesychius as the source of the "biography." The not so divine comedy began with Arethas and the scholiasts; to Arethas we can add the names of Bishop Alexander of Nicaea and Basilius of Adada.[10] The sledgehammer abuse of the scholia is very reminiscent of Suidas' phraseology. The lengthy passage of Arethas on *Jupiter Tragoedus* 47-9, and the comments on Lucian's

7. His reaction to the *Asinus* (*Cod.* 129) is echoed by the scholiast, and by Robert Graves in his Penguin version of Apuleius, 1950, p. 295.

8. See, e.g., his displeasure at the sexual element in Achilles Tatius (*Cod.* 87), and his delight in Heliodorus (*Cod.* 73). The *Vera Historia* is discussed in his account of Antonius Diogenes (*Cod.* 166); the length of this entry is notable.

9. He is hard on such blasphemers as Zosimus (*Cod.* 98) and Lucius Charinus (*Cod.* 114), and furious with Damascius (*Cod.* 130) and Clement of Alexandria (*Cod.* 109).

10. See the Teubner edition, 1906, of H. Rabe, and his papers "Die Ueberlieferung des Lukianscholia," *Nachrichten von der Gesellschaft der Wissenschaften zu Göttingen*, 1902, pp. 718-36, and "Die Lukianstudien des Arethas," ibid., 1903, pp. 643-56. There is also R. Helm's *Schol Font.*, and Winter, which latter I have not seen. For Arethas see Kougeas and N. Nilén, "Excerpta Luciana," *Symbolae Osloenses*, 1925, pp. 26-36. The subscriptions by Alexander of Nicaea are to *Vera Historia, De Calumnia, Iudicium Vocalium, Timon, Adversus Indoctum, Somnium, Hermotimus*. Basilius' contributions are on *Icaromenippus* 4; *Cataplus* 14, 24; *Convivium* 34. On Basilius see N. Festa, "A proposito di criteri per stabilire l'autenticità degli scritti compresi nel *Corpus Lucianeum*," *Mélanges Bidez*, 1934, Vol. 1, pp. 377-95.

description of Christ as a "crucified sophist," are fine examples.[11] Lucian emerges from the verbal flak as an extremely versatile villain. He is the victim of almost 40 choice epithets. Below is a list of these, with parenthetic references to the passages which evoked them. ἄθεος (*Philopseudes* 16; *Alexander* 60); ἀλαζών (*Peregrinus* 11); ἀλιτήριος (*Muscae Encomium* 7; *Philopseudes* 16; *Demosthenis Encomium* 50); βδελυρώτατος (*Hermotimus* 66); βωμολόχος (*Muscae Encomium* 7; *Vera Historia*, 2.2, 31; *Cataplus* 14; *Icaromenippus* 27; *Charon* 4; *Rhetorum Praeceptor* 17; *De Dea Syria* 60; *Saturnalia* 8; *Apology* 10); γελωτοποιός (*Saturnalia* 8; *Peregrinus* 6); γόης (*Vera Historia*, 1.17, 2.11, 31; *Jupiter Tragoedus* 28; *Charon* 4; *Rhetorum Praeceptor* 17; *Alexander* 8, 53); δαιμόνων φίλοι (*Convivium* 39); διαβολεύς (*Peregrinus* 15, 21); δυσσεβής (*Jupiter Tragoedus* 47; *Scythian* 9); ἐλεεινὸς ἄνθρωπος (*Peregrinus* 13); ἐμπαθέστατος (*De Domo* 4); ἐπάρατος (*Amores* 54); ἐπίτριπτος (*Icaromenippus* 9); ἐπιτριπτότατος (*Peregrinus* 13); κακοδαίμων (*Bis Accusatus* 14; *Lexiphanes* 15); κακὴ κεφαλή (*Muscae Encomium* 7); κατάρατος (*Jupiter Tragoedus* 47; *Vitarum Auctio* 21; *Parasitus* 41, 43; *Amores* 36; *Peregrinus* 15, 41; *De Historia conscribenda* 15); κενολόγος (*Vera Historia*, 2.43); ματαιολόγος (*De Historia conscribenda* 30); μάταιος (*Jupiter Tragoedus* 41; *Piscator* 22; *Parasitus* 6; *De Luctu* 14); ματαιότατος (*Peregrinus* 13); μεμψίμοιρος (*Apology* 10); μιαρός (*Alexander* 40; *Eunuchus* 12; *Amores* 54; *Peregrinus* 11; *De Historia conscribenda* 29); μιαρὴ κεφαλή (*Peregrinus* 13); μιαρὸς ὀνοματοθέτης (*Fugitivi* 26); μιαρολόγος (*Amores* 35); ὄλεθρος (*Saturnalia* 8; *Hermotimus* 81); ὀλέθριος (*Menippus* 22; *Peregrinus* 11); παιγνιήμων (*Lexiphanes* 4; *Vera Historia*, 2.41); παιδοφθόρος (*Convivium* 39); παμβέβηλος (*Vitarum Auctio* 15); πλαστογράφος (*Charon* 4); σκώπτης (*Peregrinus* 15, 21); ταλαίπωρος (*De Historia conscribenda* 26); ταλάντατος (*Peregrinus* 16); τερατολόγος (*Vera Historia*, 1.17; *Peregrinus* 12); τρισάθλιος (*Vitarum Auctio* 17); φιλαίτιος (*Apology* 10); χοιρώδης (*Jupiter Tragoedus* 47);

11. The Arethas passage, preserved independently in the sixteenth century *Mosquensis Gr.* 315, is edited by L. G. Westerlink in the Teubner *Arethae Scripta Minora*, 1968, Vol. 1. To do Arethas justice, he can rise above simple abuse. The scholiast threatens Lucian with "eternal hell fire," as does the closing sentence of the Suidas item.

ψωμοκόλαξ (*Icaromenippus* 27).

Lucian had done very little to deserve all this. He could not have failed to notice the Christians in the second century, and perhaps had his interest sharpened for a time by the hostile Celsus and the tolerant Galen.[12] However, the sect's appearance in the *Peregrinus* and the *Alexander* was contingent. Had the Christians not been relevant to his themes, he might never have mentioned them at all. The absence of Christ from the *Iudicium Deorum* implies that Lucian felt the cult unworthy of detailed attention or alarm. The presence of the Christians in two pamphlets attacking religious and philosophical charlatans afforded ample scope for unkind comment on their beliefs. That Lucian ignored this opportunity may be taken as proof of his lack of concern. The sexual activities of Peregrinus could easily have been linked with the common accusations against the behaviour of Christians which Fronto was happy to perpetuate.[13] One must, however, concede the possibility that Lucian was deliberately kinder to the sect than he would otherwise have been, in order to enhance the villainy of Peregrinus and Alexander.

Lucian's comments on Christianity in the *Peregrinus* are neutral and sometimes sympathetic (or condescending). They are introduced as followers of a θαυμαστὴν σοφίαν, who behaved well to their own kind, especially in times of trouble. Lucian dubs them κακοδαίμονες for believing in immortality; the epithet is not worse than neutral. The crucifixion is twice alluded to; the second of these references describes Christ as a sophist. Peregrinus is eventually expelled from the sect for eating some forbidden food, and the Christians drop out of the story.[14]

The copulation of Christians with Epicureans as enemies of Alexander is an incidental detail of Lucian's diatribe. The situation was piquant, and gains if we equate Celsus with the anti-Christian

12. For discussion and translation of the Greek and Arabic versions of Galen see Walzer, pp. 14-15.

13. The extract is preserved by Minucius Felix; see Haines 2.282, for Fronto's possible contacts with the sect.

14. See Bompaire, p. 479, and G. Bagnani, "Peregrinus Proteus and the Christians," *Historia* 4, 1955, pp. 107-12. There is an excellent bibliography in Betz.

ideologue and see both Lucian and Celsus as Epicureans. It would have been natural for both sects to oppose Alexander, and just as predictable for the prophet to whip up mob feeling against two notably unpopular sects.[15]

The *Philopatris* is irrelevant. Its authenticity was questioned as early as the scholiasts, and it is now popular to assign the piece to the reign of Nicephorus Phocas. An alternative might be to connect it with the shadowy sophist Lucian, who is addressed in a letter by the emperor Julian. Certainly, the "Galilean with receding locks and long nose, who walked on air into the third heaven," would have been congenial to that emperor.[16]

The Anti-Christ is a disappointment and a mystery. Just what provoked Arethas and his fellows to their delusion is unclear. It is tempting to make something out of the coincidence of that other Lucian of Samosata, whose career, fate, and reputation were also colourful and controversial.[17] Perhaps someone made a fatal equation between the pair, and visited the sins of the heretic on to the head of the satirist. At all events, the myth was long in developing, and enjoyed a future richer than its past.

The comparison between Lucian and Voltaire hardly stands up, unless one is disposed to disparaging the latter. Lucian was not a deep thinker, and did not pretend to be one. On his own evaluation, he was primarily an entertainer. That is merit enough in any age, and the second century was not rich in humourists (it was rich in humour, but that is another matter). Lactantius, Eunapius, and Photius were near enough to the truth. Lucian set himself up in the traditions of Aristophanes, Diogenes, and Menippus; it is notable that Demonax, to whom he consecrated an uncharacteristic eulogy, was in the same tradition. Lucian made no secret about his role, and there is no occasion for us to invent mysteries.

15. *Alexander* 25, 38.
16. *Philopatris* 12; see Macleod, Loeb *Lucian*, Vol. 8, pp. 413-14 for theories on the date of composition. *Epistle* 64 of Julian is addressed to Lucian the sophist.
17. I have no competence to judge this matter, and content myself with noting that there are 13 other Christian Lucians listed in W. Smith and H. Wace, *A Dictionary of Christian Biography*, 1882; most of these were associated with Africa.

Was he a flogger of dead horses? The notion is astonishingly absurd. It is more forgetful of simple facts than we should allow the humblest undergraduate to be. The Olympians had not been dethroned in the second century. They were still the gods of Greece and of Rome. Challenged, to be sure, by imported gods and lower superstitions. Lucian's native Syria was increasingly prominent in this field; it is amusing to speculate on how Lucian would have reacted to Elagabalus. It is convenient to say that the state religion was too remote or austere to command the genuine feelings of either intellectuals or the masses. Such clichés are impertinent and ignorant. Many in our own age have written obituaries of God, and Mr. Allegro has revived Christ in the shape of a mushroom.[18] But millions of people continue to accept Christianity, and many in the West have looked to the East for a religious as well as a communist alternative. The rituals of the Roman church are too pompous and remote for many, but it continues to show itself capable of creating converts as well as apostates. I am no apologist for Rome, but a cult which has been attractive to the Waughs and the Greenes can obviously defy the clichés. The present age also exhibits the religious compounds of the second century. Astrology and magic, black and white, are hardly defunct. Christ and Marx have been found compatible by some, and Eastern cults such as Zen jostle their Western rivals.

There is no warrant for dogmatising on other people's religious sincerity. We do not know, and never can, just how many people found the Olympians satisfactory objects of worship. Religious experience can be expressed in mass feeling, but it is also a very personal matter. Lucian either could not or would not see this. There is a tendency to assume the truth of his accounts of Peregrinus and Alexander. I have no intention of adding much to the mass of literature on these two enigmatic characters,[19] but let it at least be remembered that Lucian liked few things so much as the composition of an invective. It is rarely safe to take him as gospel truth. Demonax and Herodes also had had their differences with Peregrinus, but the rival version of Gellius (no uncritical

18. *The Sacred Mushroom and the Cross*, 1970.
19. To the usual literature add MacMullen, pp. 99-119.

admirer of all philosophers) cannot be passed over.[20] For all we can tell, the Lucian picture of Peregrinus may be a total caricature. Alexander stood in the direct tradition of Apollonius of Tyana, for whom Lucian expresses a contempt that was not universal.[21]

Contemporary justification for Lucian's religious writing is abundant. The example of Aristides is self-evident.[22] So is that of Marcus Aurelius, who expresses the ideas of his *Meditations* in the correspondence with Fronto.[23] Emperors were deified; it has been seen how Lucian passed discreet comment on the practice. Belief in magic hardly needs documentation. It may be assumed that Artemidorus had an audience for his *Oneirocritica*, and the experience of Apuleius confirms the potency of such beliefs.

Apart from Christians and Jews, Lucian took stock of the major religious phenomena of his age. The *Dialogues of the Gods* clearly can have their literary antecedents traced back beyond Plato and Xenophanes to Homer. These, and the Menippus pieces, make obvious mock of the anthropomorphic approach to religion. The theme was not new; and not exhausted.[24] The *Dialogues of*

20. Peregrinus appears twice in Gellius. In *NA* 8.3, he rebukes a young Roman knight for yawning and inattention; in *NA* 12.11, he is "virum gravem atque constantem, deversantem in quodam tugurio extra urbem (*sc.* Athens)." Anecdotes against charlatan philosophers occur in *NA* 7.2; 9.2; 10.22; 13.8; 13.24; 17.19. The gallery includes the unkempt targets of Lucian; Gellius' attitude contrasts with his respect for Favorinus and Taurus (both Platonists). The different opinions of Gellius and Herodes on Peregrinus are striking.

21. *Alexander* 5.

22. The goddess Gout was more than a match for Asclepius. Lucian frequently ridicules the cult; see, e.g., *Jupiter Tragoedus* 21, 26. The satirist is careful to play up Alexander's connections with it; see *Alexander* 10, 13, 14.

23. Haines 1.50-52; 2.246.

24. Why did Lucian select Menippus over Diogenes for his hero? Respect for another semi-Syrian? Since Lucian does not deny the inspiration of Menippus (*Bis Accusatus* 33), there is no need to follow Helm's plagiarism theories. Menippus is credited with a *Sale of Diogenes*, a necromantic piece, mock wills, mock letters from the gods, diatribes against mathematicians and grammarians, monographs on Epicurus and his followers, and other unspecified works. Strabo (16.759) dubbed him σπουδογέλοιος. The Menippan tradition in satirical literature may make the question appear superfluous. However, one wonders if Lucian knew of Diogenes Laertius' tales about

the Dead were a handy vehicle for timely jests on hero-worship
and deification; the second century was poor in neither. The
technology of religion is passed under review in the *De Luctu* and
De Sacrificiis. Astrology and the Syrian Goddess are granted mock
encomia in counterfeit Ionic.[25] Imported gods are examined in the
Iudicium Deorum; the absence of Christ from this pantheon of
natives and immigrants should again be noted. There is no
absolutely convincing explanation for Lucian's neglect of the
topic. To assume a secret respect for the cult would seem absurd,
and the notion that Christians were disqualified from review
because they did not fit the conventions of literary *Mimesis* is
unattractive. Lucian wrote within conventions, not an intellectual
straitjacket. Fronto and Celsus were capable of handling the new
topic; Marcus Aurelius and Galen also found time for the
phenomenon. I imagine that if Lucian had ever had a quarrel with
a Christian, we should have seen the latter's jacket soundly dusted.

Between gods and philosophers, though not always irrelevant
to either, comes that elusive character, the "common man."
Lucian had a good deal to say on this safe and not always
unfashionable theme. The topic is to some extent a satiric
commonplace. It will not do to adorn Lucian too eagerly with
such modern labels as "left-wing," although even the *Dialogues of
the Courtesans* have not escaped this classification.[26]

Reactions to Lucian's treatment of the theme have greatly
varied. Rostovtzeff[27] felt that "the social problem as such, the
cleavage between the poor and the rich, occupies a prominent
place in the dialogues of Lucian; he was fully aware of the

Menippus' usury; they rather tarnish the hero's integrity. Lucian clearly
wanted to create a character to stick in his audience's minds along with his
earthly Lycinus. The allusion to Menippus in Marcus Aurelius, *Meditations*,
6.47, may be a measure of his success.

25. To give the requisite Herodotean flavour; and to give Arrian and the
other relevant historiographers an object lesson in Ionic? For a detailed
commentary on the Syrian goddess see the version of H. A. Strong and J. E.
Garstang, 1913, and A. H. Harmon, Loeb *Lucian*, Vol. 5, pp. 338-411.

26. Young, p. 49: "Not an erotic book at all, but a collection of comic
anecdotes with a left-wing bias showing that whores are part of the oppressed
proletariat but can get along all right if they know the ropes."

27. Rostovtzeff, *SEHRE*, p. 621, n. 45.

importance of the problem." Bompaire,[28] by predictable contrast, wrote fearfully: "Je ne doute pas que nous ayons un jour, si elle n'existe pas déjà, une analyse marxiste de Lucien."

Some years ago, I attempted to justify Bompaire's fears by consecrating an article to the element of social satire in Lucian.[29] The presence of this element is undeniable and considerable, and I originally used it to convert Lucian into an anti-Roman writer. But second thoughts are not always inferior. Thanks both to my work on this book, and to the researches and criticisms of other scholars,[30] I know a good deal more about Lucian and his age than I did ten years ago. C. P. Jones has neatly crystallised the issue in the context of Plutarch: "To deplore aspects of Roman culture is not necessarily to be anti-Roman." I would agree with this dictum in the case of Lucian. To write about the social problems of the Antonine age did not *ipso facto* make a Greek intellectual anti-Roman. The two facets can be related, indeed should be; but they can be related in more than one way.

The force of the above distinctions, and the purpose and impact of Lucian's animadversions, can be best understood in the first instance by isolating and considering the dramatic contexts employed by the satirist. The conflict between rich and poor is the dominant motif of the 30 short *Dialogues of the Dead.*[31] An analysis of the first of these will sufficiently point the way. Diogenes commands Pollux to summon Menippus down to Hades, since the latter will find more scope for laughter down there. "Rich men, satraps, and tyrants" will be the prime targets of his ridicule. Later in the piece, Pollux is given several messages by Diogenes to take to various classes of people up on earth. The wealthy are abused for their greed and preoccupation with usury, and are warned that they will lose everything at death. Consolation is offered to the "many grieving poor" by the assurance that they may look forward to the classless society (ἰσοτιμία) which prevails in Hades.

28. Bompaire, p. 513, n. 1.
29. Baldwin 1961, pp. 199-208.
30. See Bowersock, *Sophists*, pp. 114-16; Jones, pp. 122-30, especially pp. 128-9 for Lucian.
31. See especially numbers 1, 2, 4, 10, 13, 15, 20, 21, 25, 26, 27.

This dialogue does three things. It establishes the tenor of the entire series by indicating the major themes of poverty, wealth, and the classless society of Hades; it suggests that poverty is widespread, and that the miseries of the oppressed may cause social upheaval; finally, by introducing Diogenes and Menippus as the protagonists, it connects the theme of social comment both with the cynics and with Lucian's literary *persona*.

It is worth adducing some salient points from the rest of the series. In the second of the dialogues, Menippus is busy in Hades making mock of Croesus, Midas, and Sardanapalus for their laments after their lost worldly treasures. His targets are safely dead and securely stereotyped; and they had nothing to do with Rome. The fourth has Charon and Hermes discussing the splendid deaths of the warriors of antiquity, contrasting these with the shameful deceases of present-day men who perish through gluttony or the intrigues of wives. This type of detail always presents a problem. For the reader of the *Historia Augusta* at least might divine an allusion to the death of Antoninus Pius, who expired of a surfeit of Alpine cheese, and also to the gossip concerning Marcus Aurelius' wife Faustina. Should one proceed from the timeless ethical reflection to the contemporary illustration? Or vice versa? A similar question is evoked by the group of dialogues in the series which centre about the theme of *captatio*.[32] A universal theme, but one of particular notoriety in Roman society and satire, very familiar to the readers of Juvenal, Petronius, Pliny the Younger, and Tacitus.

Other of these little dialogues rehearse jests and themes which are recurrent both in general literature and elsewhere in Lucian. The tenth exhibits Charon and Hermes again, this time loading up a quota of newly arrived dead. Pride of place is naturally given to Menippus. Less happy with their new infernal lot are a male prostitute, a Sicilian tyrant, an athlete, a general, and a philosopher. The choice of types should appeal to admirers of Sartre's *Huis Clos*. Alexander the Great is taunted with his spurious claim to divinity;[33] an obvious jest, especially coming from Lucian (using

32. *Dialogues* 5-9.
33. *Dial.* 13.

Diogenes as his mouthpiece), but one which recalls to the modern reader Vespasian's quip on his impending deification, or Dio Cassius' nice comment to the effect that Caligula learned in A.D. 41 that he was not a god. Readers of Homer will not be surprised to find Achilles unhappy in Lucian's Hades because infernal society pays no respect to military power and glory.[34] Equally discontent or demoted are wealthy philosophers such as Plato,[35] the now faded Helen,[36] and, most absurd, a poor man who regrets the loss of his earthly nothing.[37] Menippus and Diogenes, of course, adapt well to Hades; for this they are nicely commended by Cerberus — high praise from the dog to the doggy ones.[38]

The central motifs of the *Dialogues of the Dead* are developed and unified in the more ambitious *Cataplus*, *Menippus*, and *Gallus*. The parade of socially conscious gods and philosophers is twice refreshed by the introduction of the cobbler Mycillus, himself something of a stereotype.[39] Lucian's choice of setting for his dialogues may be significant. Seminars located in Hades permit an approach more universal than specifically Roman. Yet covert contemporary allusions are not thereby disqualified. And there is a double point to the choice of Menippus as the chief hero of these scenes. Along with Diogenes, he is the obvious person to typify the cynic philosophy. But his role also suggests that the social criticism of the dialogues represents the serious thought of Lucian. The satirist claims to write in the spirit of Menippus;[40] along with the recurrent Lycinus, he is a frequent vehicle for his real-life admirer.

Hades, however, is only one setting. Wealth and poverty are also the main themes of the short pieces that go under the general title of *Saturnalia*. A conversation between Cronos and his priest leads into a list of regulations for the Saturnalia, enunciated by

34. *Dial.* 15.
35. *Dial.* 20.
36. *Dial.* 18.
37. *Dial.* 27.
38. *Dial.* 21; the joke is Lucian's.
39. Cobblers were quite a commonplace in such literature; Myrtilus in the *Deipnosophistae* was the son of one.
40. *Bis Accusatus* 33.

Cronosolon. A flurry of correspondence follows: Lucian to Cronos; Cronos to Lucian; Cronos to the rich; the rich to Cronos. The poor neither send nor receive a letter; Lucian is their advocate. In his message to the god, the satirist argues that it is "most irrational" for some men to be very rich whilst others are dying of hunger. Redistribution of property on an equal basis is advocated. Cronos rejects this principle, and tries to argue that the rich are not so happy as the poor like to think. Nevertheless, though no revolutionary, he promises a reformist programme involving greater concessions by the rich. This is the burden of his subsequent letter to them; they must follow his advice in order to forestall more radical demands, and they must act quickly since the poor are already plotting against them. The rich reply, granting the concessions under protest, and grumbling that the more the poor get, the more they will want next time.

Now, the *Saturnalia* is not to be taken as an ancient *Communist Manifesto*; Lucian did not want his world torn apart, as we shall see. Yet the antagonisms between rich and poor are portrayed quite unambiguously; the arguments of both sides are provided; alternative social programmes and their implications are analysed. The use of the Roman Saturnalia as a setting for these debates is striking; it reflects an occasion which served to emphasise the injustice and inegality of normal conditions.

However, when theory threatens to give way to action, Lucian strikes a different note. A lengthy passage in the *Fugitivi*[41] has Philosophy complaining to Zeus that certain slaves and hirelings, building workers, cobblers, and the like have fled the poverty and miseries of their lot and are moving around the countryside, posing as cynics, stirring the people up to violence against their masters. And it is not only a rural phenomenon; the agitators are in all the cities.

Unfortunately, the wealth of personal detail in this dialogue suggests that Lucian is attacking specific individuals. Cantharus, the chief villain of the piece, may represent some notorious figure of the day. And the *Fugitivi* is too closely connected with the *Peregrinus* to allow impartiality on Lucian's part. But the same

41. 12-17.

basic position is taken in the *Demonax*, where Lucian's hero is praised for quelling riots.[42]

It is, then, one thing for Menippus and Diogenes to theorise about social injustice in Hades, but quite another for their latter-day followers to try and change the situation. Assessment of Lucian's position would be complicated by the *Cynicus*, if this dialogue were to be accepted as genuine. For the hispid protagonist of the piece annihilates Lycinus in debate. But this in itself is so suspicious as to reinforce the manuscript and stylistic arguments levelled against the dialogue.[43]

The armchair revolutionary, whose ardour cools rapidly when his theories are in danger of being accepted and acted upon, is a common enough phenomenon. In the context of Lucian and his age, speculation turns to romance with dangerous facility. The assumption that writers in general and satirists in particular are conditioned by their own experiences is legitimate, but of limited application. Lucian's family was not rich, but neither was it desperately poor. He certainly had ample opportunity to see poor men in Syria, Greece, and Egypt; in the last of these, he may have had dealings with some in his official capacity. There was plenty of overt social unrest in the second century. Some of this was certainly inspired or helped along by intellectual dissidents, cynics or otherwise. Lucian accused Peregrinus of instigating a revolt in Achaea; according to the *Historia Augusta*, there actually was a revolt there during the reign of Antoninus Pius.[44] One does not want to look for cynics under every bed as witch hunters have been known to do for "Reds" (Lucian tended to look for them *in* the bed, in the case of Peregrinus,[45]) but his general picture is confirmed by the golden-mouthed Dio, who depicted Alexandria as full of rabble-rousing cynics.[46] And, on the other side of the coin, Lucian's Demonax is backed up by the case of the cynic

42. *Demonax* 9.

43. See Macleod, Loeb *Lucian*, Vol. 8, 1967, p. 379.

44. *Peregrinus* 19; *HA*, *Pius* 5.5 (a revolt in Egypt is also claimed; the *HA* also has Egyptian revolts under Hadrian and Marcus Aurelius).

45. Lucian would have enjoyed the Christine Keeler-Profumo affair in England in 1963, which had a mysterious "Red" in that lady's crowded bed.

46. *Oration* 32.

Pancrates, who saved the sophist-general Lollianus from a bread riot in Athens.[47] The role of Apollonius of Tyana in the bread riot at Aspendos is also instructive; he quelled the rioters, but wrote a stinging note to the guilty merchants (who were hoarding the grain with a view to exporting it at a profit) which shamed them into supplying the people with food.[48] It will also be appreciated that bandits, strikers, and fugitives from the tax collector acted without reference to preaching cynics.[49] The situation was not of course new in the Antonine age; one need only remark that the prevalence of the theme of civic harmony and political concord in Plutarch and Dio Chrysostom is unremarkable.[50]

The sophists at large were not immune to this spectacle. It was one reason for their turning to the intellectual dream world of fourth-century Athens; and, of course, to the material comforts of their profession. Lucian's *Somnium* spoke for many. However, the sophists were not sealed off in their fantasies from the real world. We have seen that they engaged in municipal politics, represented their communities, practised law, and sometimes sought (in the case of Polemo) to calm the violence of factions. In the case of Herodes, wealth could be the cause of trouble. Lucian's attention to the issue is a refreshing, if not unique, aspect of his writing. There is no reason to deny that he had a genuine sympathy for the poor, inspired in part by his own experiences.

One doubts if the poor would have agreed with Tiresias' eulogy of their lot in the *Menippus*.[51] Lucian offered no solutions, beyond the reflection that wealth and poverty alike are transient, and he did not care to go on record as supporting violent action against the authorities. His hostility to the "radical" cynics is on a

47. Philostratus, *VS*, p. 526.

48. Philostratus, *Life of Apollonius*, 1.15; no mean feat for one who was obeying a vow of silence at the time!

49. See Baldwin 1961 for references and discussion; also MacMullen, *passim*.

50. Dio, *Orations* 24 and 27; Plutarch, *Political Precepts* (on which see Jones, pp. 110-21.

51. *Menippus* 21, where the life of the common man is said to be the best; the same sentiment is voiced at *Hermotimus* 86. Lucian's Mycillus would not have agreed!

par with the aforementioned attitude of Appian. His observations make better reading than the tissue of clichés in Aristides' *Roman Oration*, but in some measure they are clichés also. It was one thing to indicate the issue, quite another to support any "final solution" to it. For that way could lead from the relatively safe expedient of being pro-poor to the dangerous path of anti-Roman activity. It can be noted at once, in anticipation of subsequent discussion, that in his two so-called anti-Roman pieces, the *Nigrinus* and the *De Mercede Conductis*, the issue is no longer the plight of the poor, but the vulgarities of society and the shallowness of some wealthy pretenders to culture. Lucian's strictures evoke memories of Juvenal and Petronius, not comparisons with revolutionary political tracts.

There had been Greek intellectual opposition to Rome.[52] In the last generations of the Republic, Mithridates was lauded by Greeks of the order of Metrodorus, Aesopus, Heracleides, and Teucrus. There was the notable Timagenes of Alexandria, first a client then an enemy of Augustus, who came to be branded an enemy of Rome in imperial Latin literature. Our previously discussed Alexander industry was displaying political connotations, causing Livy to fulminate against Greek rhetoricians who argued that Alexander would have defeated Rome, had he lived to campaign against the West. True, the cities and countrysides of the empire were not infested with cynics, but their agitating rule was at least partly fulfilled by the manufacturers of oracles in Greek hexameters, prophesying the downfall of Rome.

All this was explicable at a time when the Republic was deservedly unpopular in the East for its maladministration, when the Parthians seemed a better horse to back than they were to be in the second century, and then when the principate was new and by no means assured of a future. Lucian's world was entirely different. The principate was secure, Rome looked invulnerable; Greece and Greeks were much more favoured. There were Romanised Greeks as well as Hellenised Romans.

Philostratus is instructive as to the possible parameters of protest. The peerless tragic actor, Clemens of Byzantium, was

52. For this see Bowersock, *Augustus*, pp. 108-111.

denied crowns of victory in Rome during the siege of Byzantium, because it was deemed treasonable to reward a fellow-citizen of a current enemy of Rome.[53] Philostratus himself rebuked the Hellenised sophist of Rome, Claudius Aelian, for cowardice in that the latter had waited until Elagabalus was dead before composing an indictment of that emperor.[54] Both anecdotes postdate Lucian, it is true; the modern reader might think that Aelian's case is no different from that of, say, Tacitus, and he will award no particular palm for moral courage to Philostratus of Lemnos; but the stories are very pertinent to the general issue.

It was more expedient to be pro-poor than anti-Roman. Lucian's claims to be an anti-Roman Greek intellectual rest on the fragile foundations of the *Nigrinus* and the *De Mercede Conductis*. The former is a pendant to the *Demonax*, and has been taken as a riposte against Aristides.[55] In fact, Nigrinus' commonplaces have a universal application, and Lucian's writings at large show no tendency to elevate the Greeks above the norms of humanity. The inspiration for the *De Mercede Conductis* could have been either personal or literary. For once, lack of a precise date is a handicap to interpretation. Was it the production of an angry young man or an embittered old one?[56] Or inspired by Juvenal? If the latter, then the pamphlet is more a retort than an imitation. Lucian's basic point is that Greek intellectuals fare badly in the households of philistine Roman millionaires. But there is more to it than that. It emerges from the pamphlet that philosophers and poets do well in these households, whilst Lucian's Syrian compatriots are only butlers.[57] Nor should it be overlooked that the intellectuals in the *Convivium* are as gross as Roman vulgarians. Moreover, in the

53. *VS*, p. 616.

54. *VS*, p. 625.

55. The chief exponent of Lucian's anti-Roman views is Peretti. See also Sherwin-White, pp. 62-86. The connection with Aristides is denied by Oliver, p. 892.

56. Macleod, Loeb *Lucian*, Vol. 8, p. 320, thinks the piece is relatively late and reflects a decline in Lucian's fortunes. The point could only be settled if we could establish the date of Lucian's tenure in Egypt.

57. *De Mercede Conductis* 10 (Syrian butlers and Libyan *nomenclatores*), 27 (reciters of erotic ditties).

larger context, Greek intellectuals did very well out of the Romans in the second century. This is not to deny that the usual dichotomy of admiration for Greek culture and detestation of contemporary Greeks was present. Imperial patronage of intellectuals was constant, but tempered. Hadrian the "Graeculus" was immediately balanced by Antoninus the "Pius"; the latter epithet is designed to recall the solider virtues. It can be recalled from an earlier discussion that victory for Avidius Cassius in 175 would have been a disaster for the sophistic profession. Superficially, at least, the *De Mercede Conductis* strikes a note as jarring as that of Juvenal's outpourings when set aside the comfortable vignettes of Pliny. Nothing seems more likely than that Lucian's animadversions were inspired by an unfortunate experience at the hands of a Roman Lord Chesterfield; alternatively, that he had been displaced from favour by a composer of erotic ditties or a long-haired philosopher.

The second century displays amusing paradoxes. The throne was occupied for nearly 20 years by a stoic philosopher who was unlikely to display the impatience of a Flavian emperor with dissentient intellectuals. Yet jokes against philosophers, and violent condemnation too, were a commonplace of the age. The impatience of Hadrian and Antoninus with some of the breed has been noticed; Lucian's attitude is matched by Gellius and Appian. The caricature of the ranting long-haired tub thumper was well established as a common literary property.

The priorities of the satirist are a mixture of inconsistency and clarity. The Platonic eunuch, Favorinus, is balanced by the worthy Nigrinus; the unspeakable Peregrinus by the admirable Demonax. Diogenes and Menippus are suffused in an odour of sanctity; their contemporary disciples are branded as hypocritical and unkempt disturbers of decency and tranquillity. Lucian has the best of both worlds. His distinction between ancient and contemporary is sustained; the point is driven home in the *Piscator*.

Personal considerations are always to be looked for in assessing his comments. The intellectual preferences of Lucian are not easy to establish. The price list of the *Vitarum Auctio* is as follows: Pythagorean (ten minas); Cynic (two obols); Cyrenaic (unsold); Democritean and Heraclitean (both unsold); Academic (two talents); Epicurean (two minas); Stoic (twelve minas); Peripatetic (20 minas); Sceptic (one Attic mina). Is the auction an instructive guide, or pure fun?[58] Isidore of Pelusium thought Lucian a cynic; set aside the *Cynicus* as spurious, and the idea is left with little support. Epicurean sentiments can be inferred from the *Alexander*, but that sect profits in his pages from its hostility to the prophet, and the tastes of Celsus may be catered to beyond the point of sincerity.[59] It is palpable that he was not a platonist, peripatetic, or stoic; Sceptic might seem an obvious label, but it would be rash to detect any special reverence for Pyrrho.[60] The tediously important *Hermotimus* reaches the same conclusion as the *Menippus*: the life of the common man is best. A rhetorical conclusion? Certainly, as noted earlier, an illogical one for Lucian;

58. This list reflects the order of appearance by the creeds. Pythagoras was an easy butt for Lucian, and followers such as Apollonius and Arignotus are roughly handled (*Alexander* 5; *Philopseudes* 29); for the contemporary nature of the theme see MacMullen, pp. 95-98, 100-14. Lucian did not have much to say about the pre-Socratic philosophers, although one imagines he found Xenophanes and Democritus (who is praised in *Alexander* 17) congenial.

59. Epicurus is warmly praised in *Alexander* 17, 25, 61; the prophet's burning of the philosopher's Κυρίαι Δόξαι (*Alexander* 47) is in a way the reverse of Peregrinus' forging of Christian books. Epicurus is commonly introduced by Lucian in Menippan roles (*Bis Accusatus* 2; *Jupiter Tragoedus* 22), and *Pro Lapsu Salutandi* 6 refers to the diction of his letters. Individual Epicureans (notably Damis in *Jupiter Tragoedus*) are frequent in Lucian's pages.

60. The Peripatetic Cleodemus is made to abuse Zeno and Cleanthes in *Convivium* 30; otherwise, Lucian has little to say about the founders of Stoicism. Comments on the sect and individual Stoics are very frequent. We would like to know what Marcus Aurelius thought about the satirist's treatment of the Stoics. The scepticism of Pyrrho, outside the *Vitarum Auctio*, is used for a light joke in *Bis Accusatus* 25 and *Icaromenippus* 25. In the gallery of philosophers in *Dialogues of the Dead* 20, Socrates gets on well with Menippus in spite (or because) of the latter's description of Plato as a flatterer of Sicilian tyrants. Alexander makes a similar criticism of Aristotle to the mocking Diogenes in *Dialogues of the Dead* 13. Lucian on Seneca would have been worth reading! However, the above passages are almost entirely comical, and it is hazardous to extract Lucian's serious opinions. I do not have the confidence of Eunapius in distinguishing the serious from the comic.

he displays sympathy for the lot of the common man but would have hated to have been thought one.

It is dangerous to infer the beliefs of a satirist from his writings. Humour on the subject of philosophers was a marketable commodity, and Lucian was commercially-minded. The situation in the second century was akin to our own. There were thinkers and preachers in high places and low. Academic vested interests are as tight as any other; the "establishment" don is not, and was not, disposed to encouraging his long-haired detractors in the lower social levels. Photius was perhaps right in concluding that Lucian believed in nothing. However, his satire on philosophy is not always to be equated with his attacks on philosophers. It must be viewed in the same light as his literary satires. Personal animosity, sectarian in-fighting, and self-advertisement form a trinity never far away from Lucian's motivation. To conclude that he believed in nothing is open to question, but is not necessarily a disappointment. The position is intellectually respectable, and perhaps men who believe in nothing are more tolerant and less dangerous than the proselyte and the converted.

The matter may be summed up in general terms. If the phrase means anything, Lucian was typical of his age. His material ambitions are explicit: fame and fortune. The extent to which he achieved them is debatable. But we need not content ourselves with mourning the lack of precise evidence. The second century was a hard and competitive age for intellectuals. There was sharp competition for preferments, and comments on a rival's career and productions were far from tepid. A profession steeped in Demosthenes was not likely to be backward in invective. It is no longer necessary to spend time criticising the rosy Gibbonian view of the age. The century was healthily torn between a variety of literary, religious, and philosophical points of view. It was a time of competing orthodoxies, not at all slumbering under one rigid creed. The controversies of men of letters reflects the social unrest and cracking military security of the period. Graeco-Roman traditions were as subject to challenge as the American Dream.

It would have been surprising if such a climate had not produced one satirist. Lucian is not only a critic of his times; he is also a compliment to them. However, the label of satirist must not be attached too glibly. He was a versatile writer. Forensic eloquence, sophistic exercises, miniature biography, comic novels, and poetry were all attempted by him. His talents for slander and abuse were matched by many. Agnosticism and some concern for the poor put him above the tattier conventions. He was adaptable within those conventions, but they were also his basis. There is no need to pontificate on his virtues or dwell on his importance in subsequent European literature. The point is to distinguish contemporary conventions from the bugbear of *Mimesis*. Lucian was the first to admit that he based his key work on classical models, and was sensible enough to admit that the label of originality was not the holy grail. But his work is not a pallid pastiche of the classics of Greek literature. Virtually all that he wrote is relevant to, and was inspired by, his own age. Topicality and universalism are quite compatible; the former is based on the latter.

Index

Greece 14, 15, 17, 28, 31, 63, 87,
104, 111, 114 f.

Hadrian 10, 15, 18, 23, 25, 42, 43 f.,
62, 63, 75, 76, 78, 82, 115
Hadrian, sophist from Tyre 46, 71,
83, 87
Harmonides 80
Hegesias 19
Heracles 9, 11, 14, 16
Hermogenes 18, 20, 59, 67
Hermotimus 11, 40, 100, 101, 112,
116
Herodes Atticus 11, 13, 15, 24, 25,
27 f., 41, 44, 45, 46, 62, 68, 72,
87, 105, 112
Herodotus 16, 92
Hesychius, of Miletus 7, 8
Hierapolis 87
Historia Augusta 16, 19, 23, 26, 28,
43, 44, 46, 75, 76, 78, 79, 88,
108, 111; and *passim* for general
"evidence."
History and Historians, contemporary
to Lucian, 75 f.
History and Historians, Greek, 88 f.
History and Historians, Roman 91 f.
Horace 13, 22

Icaromenippus 100, 101, 116
Imagines 16, 35, 95
Ionia 14, 15, 19, 64, 72, 87
Isaeus, sophist 26, 27, 71, 72
Isidore, of Pelusium 7, 98 f., 116
Italy 14, 16, 31

Iudicium Deorum 106
Iudicium Vocalium 43, 50, 57 f., 61,
100
Julian, emperor 8, 10, 23, 103
Jupiter Tragoedus 6, 9, 70, 72, 101,
105, 116
Juvenal 13, 18, 22, 26, 27, 42, 97,
113 f.

Lactantius 7, 98 f.
Laodicea 72
Lexiphanes 14, 26, 30, 36 f., 43, 47,
50 f., 55, 56, 57, 101
Libya 17
Lollianus, Avitus 18
Lollianus, sophist from Ephesus
26 f., 61, 63, 70, 73, 112
Lucian: career and chronology 7-18;
as a sophist 18-20; and emperors
22-24; and Roman dignitaries 24-
25; and Herodes Atticus 27-28;
and contemporary philosophers
28-30; and Aelius Aristides 30-
31; and Arrian, 31-33; and
Fronto 33-34; and Pollux 34-
36; and Galen 36-40; knowledge
of Latin 41-42; attitudes to
archaism and atticism 47-59;
on Greek orators and oratory 64-
69; on sophists and the sophistic
movements 70-74; on historians
and historiography 80-95; as the
"AntiChrist," 97-101; on Christians 102-3; on religion, 104-6;
attitude to Rome and the Roman
empire, 106-15; on philosophy
and philosophers 115-17
Lucian, fourth-century sophist 8,
103

Macedonia 16
Marcus Aurelius 8, 10, 11, 13, 16, 18,
19, 22, 23, 26, 28, 42, 45, 46, 62,
65, 75, 76, 85, 86, 105, 106
Marcus, sophist from Byzantium 62
Marullus 19, 22
Menippus 9, 101, 105 f., 109, 112,
116
Menippus 22, 64, 103, 105 f., 107 f.
Miletus 7, 44, 72, 82, 85
Moeris 37, 49
Muscae Encomium 101

Naples 86